How to Overcome

Managerial Shyness

and Manage Assertively

Ronald R. Johnson

Wolfgang
Press

Longwood, Florida

Wolfgang
Press

This publication is designed to provide accurate and authoritative information in regard to the subject matter covered. It is sold with the understanding that the publisher is not engaged in rendering professional services. If legal, ac-counting, medical, psychological, or any other expert assistance is required, the services of a competent professional person should be sought.

Printed in the United States of America by Creative Printing & Publishing of Sanford, FL.

ISBN 09765835-0-X

To my wife, Patricia
To my sons, Eric, Greg, and Steve
and
To my loyal friend, Titan
Thank you for your love and support

CONTENTS

The Paradox
Economic Impact
Shyness and Social Trends
Shyness and Industry Trends
Will These Trends Continue?
Corporate Responsibility
Chapter Highlights

PART II
REDUCING YOUR SHYNESS

PART III
MANAGING ASSERTIVELY

Saying No to Your Boss
Questioning Unrealistic Assignments
Questioning Inadequate Budgets
Questioning Excessive Travel
Chapter Highlights

Benefits of Corrective Feedback
Setting Expectations and Standards
Guidelines for Correcting Behavior
Correcting Punctuality Problems
Correcting Productivity Problems
Correcting Quality Problems
Correcting Negative Behavior
Progressive Discipline
Correcting Manager Behavior
Chapter Highlights

ACKNOWLEDGMENTS

Much of the inspiration to write Managerial Shyness came from reading two self-help classics: *Your Erroneous Zones*, by Dr. Wayne Dyer and *Shyness*, by Dr. Philip Zimbardo. I have adapted many of the general concepts presented in these books to business management.

In addition to the above classics, there are several recent books that have also influenced my thinking and deserve special recognition: *Shyness: A Bold New Approach*, by Dr. Bernardo Carducci; *Self-Esteem*, by Dr. Matthew McKay; and *Managing Assertively*, by Madelyn Burley-Allen.

I owe a special debt of gratitude to Garrett Johnson, Rebecca Lee-Bunka, Catherine Ochab, Kathleen Ochab, and Kathryn Reynolds. They helped me administer the Managerial Shyness Survey to hundreds of managers throughout the state of Florida. Their conscientious effort confirmed that managerial shyness was a serious subject to investigate. Thank you for sharing my vision. I could not have completed this task without your generous support.

I offer my deepest gratitude to Rusty Carpenter, my editor. Rusty helped me transform a manuscript full of ideas into a cohesive book. His suggestions were invaluable.

Finally, a special thanks to all the wonderful people at Creative Printing and Publishing. Their hard work resulted in an excellent finished product. I am especially grateful to Dave Oslin for guiding me through a maze of printing options and Holly Julien for her patience and expertise during layout and graphic design.

Longwood, Florida   RRJ

January, 2005

Introduction

Shyness is common and widespread in our society. Stanford University conducted pioneering research on shyness back in the 1970s and discovered that over 40% of Americans considered themselves shy. Recent research by Indiana State University indicates that the percentage of Americans who now consider themselves shy has increased to nearly 50%.

Shyness is also common and widespread in management. My research indicates that approximately one out of five managers exhibit shy characteristics significant enough to adversely impact their job performance. This managerial shyness is common in both males and females, and at all levels of management.

Every day hundreds of employees with shy characteristics are promoted to supervisory positions. Eventually, management discovers that many of these supervisors are having difficulty performing routine supervisory functions such as assigning unpleasant tasks, denying unreasonable requests, and correcting employee behavior. In an attempt to change this passive behavior, many of these supervisors are sent to assertive management training. However, one and two-day training classes in managing assertively will not transform a shy person into an assertive manager. A more comprehensive approach is required for this task. And that is the objective of this book.

This book is divided into three parts. In Part I, the emphasis is on understanding what managerial shyness is all about.

1

Chapter one introduces you to the paradox of managerial shyness. It explains why companies offer supervisory positions to shy employees, and more importantly, why shy employees accept them. It discusses social trends and shyness, as well as the economic impact of managerial shyness. And, it calls for companies to assume more responsibility in identifying and developing shy managers.

Chapter two explains how managerial shyness spans a wide psychological continuum and can vary from occasional feelings of nervousness to overwhelming anxiety. It outlines the primary characteristics of managerial shyness, and introduces you to the four major types of managerial shyness.

Part II focuses on ways to reduce your shyness. These chapters offer specific techniques to help you develop positive thinking, build self-esteem, develop self-confidence, and enhance social skills.

Chapter three teaches you how to change your behavior and take control of your life. It reminds you that you control your thoughts, and your feelings come from your thoughts. Therefore, you have the power to control your thoughts and your shy feelings.

Chapter four gives you the opportunity to take the Managerial Shyness Survey. This self-assessment allows you to take an honest look at yourself and objectively measure your managerial shyness. In addition, this survey provides a baseline that can be used to monitor your progress in reducing your shyness.

Chapter five shows you how to improve your self-esteem. Shyness researchers have consistently found a significant correlation between shyness and low self-esteem. This chapter discusses the origin of self-esteem and describes the rewards for self-denunciation. It also teaches you how to stop self-denunciation and eliminate your need for approval.

Chapter six teaches you how to develop your self-confidence. While self-esteem centers on self-worth, self-confidence deals with the ability to make decisions and take risks. This chapter describes the origin of self-confidence and discusses the importance of learning how to take risks.

Chapter seven equips you with the tools to improve your social skills. Shy people avoid social encounters because they have never learned how to meet people, start conversations, and speak up in groups. This chapter shows you how to make small talk, participate in meetings, make presentations, and participate in interviews.

Part III concentrates on managing assertively. These chapters focus on asking for what you want, learning how to say no, and correcting employee behavior.

Chapter eight teaches you how to ask your employees for what you want. It discusses the art of delegation, and shows you how to project physical assertiveness, assign unpleasant tasks, and avoid reverse delegation. In addition, this chapter presents powerful techniques for asking your peers, and your boss, for what you want.

Chapter nine helps you learn how to say no to your employees. It outlines effective guidelines for saying no, and shows you how to deny salary requests, schedule changes, and unreasonable perks. Also, this chapter presents effective techniques for saying no to your peers and your boss.

Chapter ten teaches you how to correct employee behavior. It discusses the benefits of corrective feedback and the importance of setting expectations and standards. In addition, this chapter presents effective guidelines for correcting behavior and shows you how to correct punctuality, productivity, and quality problems.

Chapter eleven paints a brief portrait of the assertive manager. It summarizes the objectives of each chapter and reminds you that your journey is not over. Reducing your shyness and increasing your assertiveness is a lifelong project.

Take your time reading these chapters and doing the exercises. Read each chapter carefully and absorb the contents fully. Each chapter reinforces the concepts from the previous chapter and builds on that information. After you have read several chapters and successfully completed the exercises, you will notice repetition of key ideas. This designed repetition is necessary to alter your thinking and your behavior. Crucial themes must be repeated again and again until you fully understand and accept the concepts. Only then will you start to alter your behavior.

If you really want to reduce your shyness and become an assertive manager, you must commit yourself to the self-improvement exercises contained in this book. Simply reading the exercises is not enough. And, doing only the exercises that seem interesting is not enough. You must do all of the exercises if you want to change your behavior.

Change is possible. An enormous body of research exists to support the conclusion that human personality and behavior are quite changeable. I suffered through 35 years of shyness before I discovered that I had the power to control my thoughts, and change my behavior. Much of my personal and professional success comes from practicing the suggestions outlined in this book. I use them every day.

Now it's time for you to take control of your thoughts and change your behavior. Change is not easy, and it does not come fast. Every fiber in your body will resist your attempt to change. It requires a tremendous amount of hard work to unlearn all the self-defeating thoughts that you have assimilated during your life. If you have realistic expectations, and are persistent in your quest for a better life, you can reduce your shyness and become an assertive manager.

PART I
UNDERSTANDING MANAGERIAL SHYNESS

THE SHY MANAGER

Mark walked down the long hallway, entered the conference room, and sat down. As usual, his heart was pounding, his hands were shaking, and his mouth was dry. Although his project was on schedule, and within budget, he dreaded these weekly staff meetings. As he glanced around the room, waiting for the meeting to start, many thoughts raced through his mind. "What do the other managers think about me?" "Will I be able to answer their questions?" "Does my boss think I'm doing a good job?" "Will I be able to answer his questions?"

Mark was labeled "shy" early in his childhood. He was tall, skinny, and had a face full of freckles. He was a good student in elementary school, but avoided class discussions and group activities. His mother drove him to school every morning and picked him up every afternoon. She felt there was too much pushing and shoving on the school bus, and riding a bicycle was way too dangerous. He was allowed to have friends over after school, but his mother rarely allowed him to visit other children's homes. She worried about his safety and didn't want anything bad to happen to her "shy little boy."

In high school Mark excelled in academics, particularly math, and spent most of his free time on computers. He had no interest in sports and avoided school clubs and organizations. Although Mark had a few friends, he was extremely self-conscious in all social situations. In college he majored in computer science and graduated in the top five percent of his class. Shortly after graduation he married his college sweetheart, Beth, and went to work for a software development firm in California. The first three years were smooth sailing. Mark established himself as an outstanding programmer. In the beginning of his fourth year, Mark was promoted to manage a new software project. To prepare him for this new responsibility, his company sent him to a three-day course for new supervisors.

Although increased salary and stock options were strong motivators, Mark soon discovered that he was uneasy in this new role. He suffered extreme anxiety in management meetings and was afraid to ask questions or speak up. He was uncomfortable giving work assignments, and procrastinated when he had to correct employee behavior.

Mark is a "shy manager." And, he is not alone. During my management career I witnessed many shy employees like Mark struggle with management responsibility. Some, after experiencing psychological and/or physical problems, eventually resigned, requested demotions, or were terminated. Others sought additional management training, self-help books, and counseling. In time, many of these managers increased their self-confidence and became more comfortable in their management role. Unfortunately, some shy managers decided to remain in their positions, and not seek help. In so doing, they sentenced themselves to a career of psychological pain and suffering.

How prevalent is *managerial shyness*? More than you would expect. During the past several years, I have surveyed hundreds of managers in many diverse industries. The results of the survey are shocking. Approximately *one out of five* managers exhibit shy characteristics significant enough to adversely impact their job performance. The survey also shows that shy-

8

ness is common in both males and females, and at all levels of management. You will have an opportunity to take the Managerial Shyness Survey when you reach Chapter 4.

THE PARADOX

Managerial shyness is indeed a *paradox*. The words "shy" and "manager" seem so contradictory. How can a manager be shy? Managers must be assertive and self-confident. They must make effective presentations and sell their ideas to upper management as well as their employees. They must feel comfortable giving orders, monitoring employee activity, and correcting employee behavior. And, they must interact and communicate daily with their employees to build group morale. Being assertive and self-confident in all these critical areas is quite a challenge for someone who is shy.

Why do shy employees become managers? Although many shy employees have strong reservations about management responsibility, one of the main reasons they accept promotions is money. Management positions offer increased salary, stock options, bonuses, increased leave time, improved retirement plans, and many other attractive fringe benefits. Many shy men and women reluctantly accept more responsibility to improve the standard of living for their families.

Another reason that shy employees accept management responsibility is their inability to say "no." Most shy people have low self-esteem and self-confidence and a very strong need for approval. It is very difficult for a shy person to say "no" to someone in a position of authority. Many shy employees are convinced that management will no longer "like them" if they decline supervisory responsibility, and some actually believe they might be terminated if they refuse the promotion. Whatever the case, many employees believe that they can overcome their shyness and become effective managers if given the chance.

Why do organizations offer shy employees management positions? In some cases, management does not know the employee is shy. Employees are able to conceal their symptoms of shyness much of the time. In other situations, shy employees are promoted because they are excellent workers who don't "rock the boat." Sometimes the managers who promote them are shy themselves and prefer to have supervisors who are not aggressive or threatening. A shy top management executive of a large grocery chain told me the secret of his success, "I stood back and watched everyone else eliminate themselves."

The culture of the organization also plays an important role in the selection process for supervisors and managers. Shy employees are usually not considered strong candidates in an organizational culture that embraces hierarchical management philosophy and aggressive management styles. On the other hand, shy employees are viable candidates in an organization that encourages participative management and consensus decision-making. Organizations with promotion policies based largely on seniority, such as government agencies, also provide the shy employee an excellent opportunity for management responsibility.

Shy employees have a strong dependency on the organization, and a strong loyalty to the organization. They value the security of their present employment and usually do not look for greener pastures. Management gives these factors considerable weight when considering someone for a promotion.

ECONOMIC IMPACT

Shy managers cause lower productivity in organizations for several reasons. First, shy managers have trouble exercising authority over their employees. They worry too much about their employees' feelings and not enough about the work to be performed. Therefore, they are reluctant to monitor employee performance and correct negative employee behavior. The result is lower productivity from the employee. Second, shy managers lack the social skills to interact comfortably with their employees to build camaraderie and teamwork. This ultimately leads to low morale and high turnover. Third, shy managers have lower productivity themselves than assertive managers. They doubt their ability to make decisions and solve problems, and rarely offer suggestions or new ideas to improve work methods.

Managerial shyness costs corporate America *billions* of dollars a year in lost productivity. According to the U.S. Bureau of Labor Statistics there are over 20 million managers in America. And, based on the results of my research, a significant percentage of them are shy. Considering the large number of managers, and the prevalence of shyness, the economic impact of this problem is staggering.

In addition to lost productivity, shyness also causes lost opportunities for many individuals and society as a whole. Many intelligent and gifted people never become business or government leaders because shyness undermines their ability to successfully interact and influence people. It is a tragedy that so many gifted people never realize their potential due to shyness. The cost is high for the individual, but even higher for society.

SHYNESS AND SOCIAL TRENDS

Shyness, *the abnormal fear of people*, is a puzzling personality trait. Although there is no universally accepted definition of shyness, most psychologists agree that shy people experience discomfort and behavioral inhibition in the presence of others. Hence, shyness is characterized by an avoidance of social contact. Shy people worry about their appearance. They worry about their speech. And, they worry about their performance. In general, shy people worry about how others will perceive them, especially in unfamiliar and uncontrollable situations. Therefore, many shy people follow strict daily routines in order to reduce the uncertainty in their lives.

Shyness is complex and difficult to define. However, Dr. Philip Zimbardo, founder of the Stanford University Shyness Clinic, has identified several general characteristics of shyness. First, there are the outward behavior signs like avoidance of eye contact and reluctance to talk. Second, there are the physiological symptoms of nervousness and anxiety, such as blushing, perspiration, and tremors. And third, there is an overwhelming feeling of self-consciousness or preoccupation with self. These general characteristics of shyness will be applied to managerial shyness in the next chapter.

Shyness spans a wide psychological continuum. It can vary from occasional feelings of nervousness to overwhelming anxiety. At one end of the continuum are those who occasionally feel awkward in the presence of others, especially in unfamiliar situations. They may blush or become tongue-tied when meeting a new person, particularly an authority figure. At the other end of the shyness continuum are those individuals who are chronically shy. They have an extreme fear of people and have sentenced themselves to a life of social isolation.

Shyness is often confused with introversion. Although introverts have the self-esteem and social skills necessary for interacting with others, they prefer being by themselves. On the other hand, shy people want to interact with others but lack the necessary self-esteem and social skills.

Shyness is common and widespread in our society. Dr. Philip Zimbardo conducted pioneering research on shyness at Stanford University back in the 1970s. He discovered that over 40% of Americans considered themselves shy. Recent research by Dr. Bernardo Carducci, Director of the Shyness Research Institute at Indiana State University Southeast, indicates that the percentage of Americans who now consider themselves shy has increased to nearly 50%. Why is shyness so widespread? And, why does it appear to be increasing in our society?

One reason is the continuing *erosion* of the family unit. With skyrocketing divorce rates, our society is now at a point where one out of two marriages ends in divorce. Children frequently blame themselves for their parent's divorce and often experience anxiety, depression, or loss of self-esteem. Shyness researchers have consistently found a significant correlation between shyness and low self-esteem. In addition, the percentage of households where both parents work has been steadily increasing over the past 30 years. In many households today, both parents are career oriented and prefer to work. In other households, both parents have to work to meet financial obligations. In either case, parents have less time to spend developing their children's self-esteem and self-confidence. They come home after work and must cook, clean, do laundry, and perform many other household tasks. In addition, working parents are tired and stressed when they come home and are often critical of their children's behavior. You will learn in Chapter 5 that critical parents lay the foundation for low self-esteem and shyness.

Another reason that shyness is so prevalent in our society is the low priority it receives in our educational system. Although many elementary schools offer an array of special needs programs, shyness is usually not included. Many school administrators believe that shyness should be addressed in the home. In addition, rather than help shy students to be more assertive, teachers often reinforce shyness. "Bobby is so shy and well-behaved. He never causes any trouble. He always does what I ask. It is such a joy to have him in my class." With many teachers focusing their time and energy on aggressive problem students, shy students often get lost in the classroom. Unfortunately, this continues into higher education.

By the time shy students reach middle school and high school they are labeled "shy" by their peers. They are often snubbed by popular student groups and often excluded from social functions. During this time many shy students begin to compensate for their lack of social skills by pursuing academic excellence.

Much of the college experience continues to reinforce shyness. Most colleges are large and impersonal and provide an excellent environment for the shy student to get lost in the crowd. Students spend many hours alone reading vast amounts of literature, writing research papers, and studying for exams. Shy students avoid social interaction by devoting more time to study. This leads to better grades and the pattern of avoidance is reinforced. *The end result is reduced social skills and reinforced shyness.*

A third reason that shyness is increasing in our society is technology. Dr. Bernardo Carducci, a leading shyness researcher, feels the electronic revolution in the home has caused *increased family isolation.* Twenty years ago many families regularly attended, and participated, in community activities. Today, mom is on the Internet reading her e-mail, researching possible vacation sites, and shopping for the best book prices. Dad is busy on another computer checking bank accounts, looking at new cars, and buying and selling stocks. One child is simulating a jet flight on a video game station, while the other child is building a roller coaster using computer-aided-design software. And, everyone is drawn to instant messaging. There are several problems with this picture. First, the whole family is spending more time at home and less time in the community. In addition, family members are spending more time on individual electronic activities and less time on family group activities. Although Internet chat rooms appear to make social contact easier for the shy, it's also very convenient to *hide* behind the Internet and use it as an *excuse* to avoid meeting people in the traditional face-to-face manner.

As people satisfy more of their needs within the home, they lose their need for human contact. They prefer shopping online rather than going to busy stores. They wait for a movie to come out on video rather than dealing with crowds at the theater. They become accustomed to the anonymity of e-mail. Ultimately, many people lose interest in their social life or activities outside the home. The less time they spend with others, the less confident they become with people due to the absence of face-to-face contact. The outcome, once more, is reduced social skills and reinforced shyness.

SHYNESS AND INDUSTRY TRENDS

Shyness is also common, widespread, and growing in industry. Based on my experience and research, I estimate that millions of managers in America are shy. And, this number is increasing every year due to several factors. First, as previously noted, the percentage of shy people in the general population is increasing. Second, and most obvious, the total work force, including managers, is increasing. Third, due to increased "employee rights" legislation and lawsuits, management has become more receptive to selecting "non-aggressive" employees to become supervisors. Many of these "non-aggressive" employees are shy. Fourth, and most important, many research studies indicate *that shy people gravitate toward science and engineering careers.* And, the U.S. Bureau of Labor Statistics reports that science and engineering jobs grew *three times faster* than total civilian jobs during the past twenty years. In addition, many shy scientists and engineers are promoted to management positions. The case study involving Mark at the beginning of this chapter is an excellent example of this trend.

Science and engineering education is very demanding. Only the top students in the country are admitted into these programs. Students must have excellent test scores and grades. To be successful in these programs, students must maintain high grades and spend a considerable amount of time reading and studying. Based on my experience and research, I believe that many shy students are attracted to science and engineering, and the excessive demands of these programs also reinforce shyness. During my tenure as a university professor, I had the opportunity to observe and interact with thousands of undergraduate and graduate students. In general, science and engineering students were noticeably shyer than other students. Many sat in the back of the class and rarely participated in class discussions. During meetings in my office, many exhibited the general characteristics of shyness. They avoided eye contact, were reluctant to talk, and displayed physiological symptoms of nervousness such as blushing, perspiration, and tremors.

I also had the opportunity to observe and interact with hundreds of managers during my career in the computer industry. Engineering managers were noticeably shyer than sales, marketing, and manufacturing managers. Many avoided eye contact, were reluctant to talk in meetings, and exhibited physiological symptoms of nervousness in interpersonal situations.

Much of the job growth during the past twenty years has been in high-tech industries such as electronic components, computers and peripherals, software, telecommunications, biotechnology, pharmaceuticals, and healthcare. Many of the new jobs created in these high-tech industries were science and engineering positions. New scientists were required to staff the expanding research laboratories in biotechnology and pharmaceuticals. New electrical and mechanical engineers were hired to fill the mushrooming product development departments in the computer and telecommunications industries. And, new industrial and manufacturing engineers were added to design and implement advanced automation and robotic systems in virtually every industry. A large percentage of these scientists and engineers were shy, and many were promoted to management positions.

WILL THESE TRENDS CONTINUE?

Will the family unit continue to erode in our society? Or, will parents rediscover commitment, loyalty, and family values? Will they begin to place a higher priority on developing their children's self-esteem and self-confidence? A very wise professor once told me, "The future can't be predicted – it can only be invented." There are many dedicated people working very hard to increase public awareness of the problems associated with the erosion of the family unit. During the past few years many excellent books and articles have been published on the importance of developing self-esteem and self-confidence in children. Much of this information has been communicated to parents through publications, seminars, and talk shows. Although public awareness is growing, the information is only reaching a very small percentage of the population. Therefore, unless the exposure can be dramatically increased, I do not see a significant change in this trend in the near future.

Will our educational system continue to reinforce shyness? Will more teachers and administrators start to recognize the importance of addressing shyness at an early age? Although some teachers and administrators are becoming more empathetic toward the shy student, I'm afraid many will continue to place higher priorities on other educational issues. However, in the long run, addressing shyness issues at school may not be relevant. There is a growing trend toward online education in the home. Politicians and school administrators will embrace this solution to help relieve the crowding at existing schools and prevent the construction of new ones. Most colleges now offer many courses online. This trend will extend downward to high schools, middle schools, and even elementary schools.

Rapidly changing job requirements for occupations in science and technology will continue to challenge our university system to meet the demand. Student competition for excellent universities will intensify. Students will have to study even harder to succeed in the new professional specialty fields. And, increased use of technology in the learning process will continue to reduce the need for face-to-face social interaction. Therefore, the end result will continue to be reduced social skills and reinforced shyness.

Technology in the home will not stop. We have only seen the tip of the iceberg in home electronics. The Internet is not a fad—it is here to stay. The economic downturn in 2001 weeded out the weak players, but the e-commerce infrastructure is alive and well. Families will continue to spend more time at home performing business, social, educational, and entertainment functions online. Every member of the family will have a personal computer and a high-speed data link to the Internet. Parents will spend less time in the office and more time working at home. They will also spend less time in stores and more time shopping at home. Children will spend less time in the classroom and more time at home taking courses on the Internet. Video games will continue to become more realistic with faster computer processors and higher-resolution graphics. And, the home entertainment market will take a giant leap forward with the introduction of affordable, full-motion, personal simulators. Now children will really be able to fly airplanes, drive race cars, and ride roller coasters.

The U.S. Bureau of Labor Statistics projects continued rapid growth in science and engineering occupations for the next ten years. High-tech industries will continue to expand, and traditional industries will continue to automate all phases of their operation. Electronic components, E-commerce, pharmaceutical, healthcare, and biotechnology will exhibit exceptionally strong growth rates.

In summary, social trends in family stability, education, and home technology will continue to reduce social skills and reinforce shyness. Millions of shy employees will be promoted to fill new management positions. And, billions of dollars will be lost in productivity, *unless corporate America assumes more responsibility for developing shy managers.*

CORPORATE RESPONSIBILITY

In addition to traditional management training, corporations must assume more responsibility for identifying and developing shy managers. *One and two-day training classes in managing assertively will not transform a shy person into an assertive manager.* A comprehensive development program is required for this task. This program must be custom tailored to each individual, and should focus initially on self-awareness, building self-esteem, and developing self-confidence. After successfully completing these prerequisites, managers should then be taught effective social skills and techniques for managing assertively. Each of these topics should become an integrated building block in a total development program.

Corporations have many types of training and development programs: quality assurance, customer relations, cultural diversity, sexual harassment, time management, stress management, aggression in the workplace, etc. The list is endless. Perhaps it's time for corporations to take a close look at managerial shyness.

Many shy employees can become good managers if they participate in an effective management development program, *and they really want to change their behavior.* Although most of this chapter has focused on the negative aspects of shyness, there is a positive side to shyness. Shy people are perceived as modest and reserved, while aggressive people are often considered obnoxious and pretentious. Shy people are also discreet and introspective. They do not intimidate or hurt others as aggressive people may do. Shy people are also good listeners and can understand both sides of a dispute.

Shy employees, after effective development, can overcome their shyness and become good managers. They will be good listeners, and their employees will not be afraid to come to them with their problems. They will be reserved and discreet, and work well with their peers. They will carefully consider all alternatives and will not make rash decisions. And, they will be loyal to their managers and the organization.

You have learned in this chapter that managerial shyness is a growing problem in America, and corporations must accept more responsibility for the development of shy managers. In the next chapter, you will discover that managerial shyness is a very *misunderstood* and *complex* personality trait.

CHAPTER HIGHLIGHTS

- Managerial shyness is prevalent in industry. The Managerial Shyness Survey indicates that approximately one out of five managers exhibit shy characteristics.

- Although many shy employees have strong reservations about management responsibility, one of the main reasons they accept promotions is increased salary and fringe benefits.

- Another reason that shy employees accept management responsibility is their inability to say "no." Most shy people have low self-esteem and self-confidence, and a very strong need for approval. It is very difficult for a shy person to say "no" to someone in a position of authority.

- Managerial shyness has a major economic impact in America. Shy managers cause lower productivity in organizations. This lost productivity costs corporate America billions of dollars a year.

- Shyness is common and widespread in our society. The percentage of Americans who now consider themselves shy has increased to nearly 50%.

- Shyness is increasing in our general population due to (1) the continuing erosion of the family unit, (2) the low priority it receives in our educational system, and (3) the increased use of technology in the home.

- Shyness is also increasing in management because of changing job trends. The demand for scientists and engineers has exploded during the past twenty years, and shy people tend to gravitate toward these careers. Many of these shy scientists and engineers are promoted to management positions.

- Corporations must assume more responsibility for identifying and developing shy managers. One and two-day training classes in managing assertively will not transform a shy person into an assertive manager.

- Corporations need to develop custom tailored programs that include modules on self-awareness, self-esteem, self-confidence, social skills, and assertive management.

- Shy employees can become good managers if they participate in an effective management development program and they really want to change their behavior.

2

THE MANY FACES OF SHYNESS

Most of us have encountered shyness in our daily lives—becoming tongue-tied in a job interview, getting "butterflies" in our stomach before a presentation, and feeling our heart pound when asking for a raise. Shy tendencies are common because it's normal to be cautious—to fear rejection and want acceptance. When does this normal reaction become a *debilitating* personality trait?

THE SHY CONTINUUM

Managerial shyness, like shyness in general, spans a wide psychological continuum and can vary from occasional feelings of nervousness to overwhelming anxiety. Many managers experience dry mouth, "butterflies," perspiration, or heart palpitations before an important presentation. This is a normal reaction. In fact, I believe a person makes a better presentation if they are a bit nervous.

The middle range of shyness includes managers who *frequently* feel intimidated and awkward in certain situations with certain types of people. Their discomfort is strong enough to disrupt their routine and inhibit their required functions. Managers in this middle range of shyness are usually shy because they lack self-confidence, social skills, and techniques for managing assertively. They don't know how to speak up in meetings or correct employee behavior. Their blushing, sweating, and stuttering are so excessive, and obvious, that the audience focuses on the shyness rather than the presentation.

No two shy managers are alike. One may have extreme difficulty in correcting employee behavior, but feel very comfortable speaking to groups. Another may agonize over public speaking and be very effective in administering employee discipline. I once worked with a young manager who made outstanding presentations to large audiences, but could not talk to a small group without blushing and stuttering. Apparently, he perceived the large audiences to be impersonal and not as threatening as the small groups.

Chronically shy managers are at the far end of the shyness continuum. They have an *extreme* fear of people and are *incapacitated* by overwhelming anxiety. They stay in their office most of the time and delegate much of their supervisory responsibility to a subordinate. These managers also adhere to strict, regimented routines in order to reduce the uncertainty and risk in their daily lives.

CHARACTERISTICS OF MANAGERIAL SHYNESS

The three general characteristics of shyness also apply to managerial shyness. First, shy managers avoid eye contact and are reluctant to talk. They have a disposition to remain silent and not speak up. They hesitate to correct employee behavior because they fear rejection, and they want their employees to like them. Ironically, they are doing their employees a disservice. Most employees want to know if they are doing something wrong so they can correct it.

Shy managers are also reluctant to speak up in staff meetings. They fear rejection from their peers and others in management positions. *Shy managers pay a high price for this silence.* Many of their ideas and opinions are never factored into the decision making process. They have to live with decisions they don't support. In some cases, these decisions cause them to become overburdened with tasks that aren't their responsibility. In other cases, they are asked to complete tasks by unrealistic deadlines. Their inability to speak up and say "no" often results in failure to meet required deadlines and bosses who are disappointed with their performance. This failure to meet unrealistic deadlines also causes low morale for their employees and a loss of confidence in their manager.

In addition to their unwillingness to speak, some shy managers simply avoid people whenever possible. They prefer the detachment of e-mail to personal meetings. Using the computer as a shield, they avoid the emotional threat of human contact and the uncertainty of live feedback. Some people *mistakenly* mislabel shy managers as aloof, conceited, snobby, or stuck-up, because they appear to be distant and unfriendly. To the contrary, shy managers are simply "afraid of people." This non-rational fear is one of the most puzzling aspects of human behavior.

The second general characteristic of managerial shyness, the physiological symptoms of anxiety, covers a wide range of *physical stress reactions.* They include blushing, trembling, upset stomach, dry mouth, perspiration, clammy hands, faintness, and heart palpitations. Most of us have experienced these stress reactions sometime in our lives. We accept them as mild discomfort and look to the positive aspects of what might happen later—getting a raise from the boss, selling our idea to the staff, or receiving a standing ovation from the audience. However, shy managers tend to *concentrate* on these physical symptoms.

When making a presentation, they fear they will blush. And they do! When conducting an employee evaluation, they fear their hands will tremble. And they do!

Some stress reactions, like upset stomach and heart palpitations, can be concealed. Others, like blushing and perspiration, are more difficult to hide. Sometimes the stress reactions become so overwhelming that they interfere with the mind. Shy managers may lose track of their thoughts during a presentation or not hear a person's name during an introduction. If the manager continues to dwell on the stress reactions, they can become long-term, out-of-control panic attacks.

The third general characteristic of managerial shyness is *self-consciousness*. Self-awareness and self-analysis are important to maintaining a healthy personality. However, many shy managers are *obsessed* with the self-analysis of their thoughts and feelings. This characteristic manifests itself in both a public and a private dimension. *Publicly shy managers* are concerned about their awkward behavior and appearance in social situations. They constantly ask themselves:

- "Do my employees like me?"

- "What do the other managers think about me?"

- "Does my boss think I'm doing a good job?"

- "Will the audience like my presentation?"

- "Did I make a good impression at the staff meeting?"

- "Do my employees like my management style?"

- "Is my boss upset with me because I was so quiet in the meeting?"

- "Was I dressed too casual for the meeting?"

Unlike publicly shy managers, *privately shy managers* project an image of composure and confidence. They hide their anxiety using well-learned social skills and carefully plan their personal interactions in advance. However, inside their minds, nervous energy soars, and their thoughts race out of control.

Privately shy managers are more concerned with *feelings* than *behavior*. They focus inward and their obsessive self-analysis becomes an end in itself. They are always trying to figure themselves out and are constantly examining their mood, motivation, and sense of worth:

- "It seems that I'm always depressed. Maybe it's time to change jobs."

- "I'll never get that promotion. Maybe I have a bad attitude."

- "I wonder if I should be more assertive in the staff meetings."

- "Maybe I should have prepared more for the presentation."

- "I can't believe they promoted me. I really didn't deserve it."

- "They will be hard to convince. I don't think I can do it."

- "The more I think about the meeting, the more nervous I get."

- "I can't believe we came in second. Maybe I should have pushed the team harder."

Notice that each of these thoughts has one thing in common—*negativity. Privately shy managers are their own worst critics.* They expect perfection from themselves and their employees, and are satisfied by nothing less. They are often perceived by their peers and employees as "slave drivers."

Although privately shy managers are harder to detect, they share the same insecurities and lack of self-confidence as publicly shy managers. They do an excellent job of playing the role of manager. However, when they are placed in an unfamiliar situation, they may exhibit the same silence and physical stress reactions as publicly shy managers.

THE PUBLICLY SHY MANAGER

Mary is a 28 year-old nurse who has worked in a metropolitan hospital for the past six years. Mary was recognized early in her career for her outstanding commitment to quality in patient care. She would always go the extra mile for every patient under her care. Wanting to instill Mary's work ethic in more nurses, management promoted Mary to supervisor. She reluctantly accepted the position after persistent pressure from several hospital managers. Mary always had a difficult time saying "no" to people in positions of authority. Concerned about her shyness, Mary was very apprehensive about her new position.

Mary wanted her employees to like her. She frequently approved time off for nurses even when the shift was short. She would cover their assignments and then work additional hours to finish her supervisory paperwork. Mary was also afraid to ask her nurses to do unpleasant tasks. In many cases she would do them herself. In addition, Mary was reluctant to discipline her nurses because she didn't want to hurt their feelings. Rather than deal with these problems assertively, Mary would often remain silent and look the other way. Mary always gave good evaluations to her nurses—even some who didn't deserve it. Once again, she was afraid to hurt their feelings and wanted all of her employees to like her.

As part of her supervisory responsibilities, Mary was occasionally asked to teach classes on quality in patient care. These classes were attended by several departments and could contain up to 100 nurses. Mary dreaded these classes because she blushed and stuttered during the presentations. One class was especially bad. She had an extremely dry mouth, but was afraid to pick up a glass of water. She didn't want anyone to see her hand trembling. The more she thought about her trembling hand, the worse it got. Finally, she gave the class a break, and went down the hall to a water fountain.

Mary suffered from shyness her whole life. She suffered in school, at social events, and work. Although she had always been able to cope in the past, this new supervisory responsibility was too threatening and painful. She eventually asked for a demotion and returned to floor nursing.

Publicly shy managers, like Mary, have low self-esteem and lack self-confidence. In addition, many have never been given the opportunity to learn effective social skills and techniques for managing assertively. Their heightened fear of rejection and failure cripples their effectiveness as managers. Publicly shy managers are often:

- Apprehensive about correcting employee behavior

- Reluctant to ask employees to do unpleasant tasks

- Afraid to deny unrealistic requests

- Hesitant to give low evaluations when warranted

- Reluctant to ask questions in staff meetings

- Apprehensive about expressing ideas
  and wants in staff meetings

- Afraid to say "no" to unrealistic assignments and/or deadlines

- Afraid to ask for a raise or promotion

- Hesitant to ask for additional resources like personnel or equipment

- Reluctant to ask peers for information or help

- Apprehensive about giving presentations

- Apprehensive about holding staff meetings with their employees

- Reluctant to set expectations and limitations for their employees

- Hesitant to give positive feedback (strokes) to their employees

- Inclined to procrastinate and postpone decisions

The above passive behaviors have a devastating effect on employees and the organization. The devastating effects include:

- Increased employee conflicts

- Reduced cooperativeness and teamwork

- Increased late assignments

- Reduced enthusiasm, motivation, and morale

- Increased absenteeism and turnover

- Decreased productivity

THE PRIVATELY SHY MANAGER

John is a 32 year-old marketing executive for a Fortune 500 company. During college he was a well-known athlete and very popular on campus. On the outside, this handsome student radiated poise and self-confidence, but on the inside, John was haunted by insecurity and doubt. His thoughts frequently turned inward to the self-analysis of his shy moods. He was constantly baffled by this paradox. On the one hand, he felt that he had always been outgoing and extroverted, but on the other, he knew that he was shy.

After completing college, John went to work for a large electronics company. In two years he advanced from a junior account representative to senior account manager. His sales presentations were well rehearsed and delivered with impressive confidence. John always exceeded his sales quotas and was quickly promoted to district sales manager. Sales in John's district far surpassed the other districts, but John's employees paid the price. John was a perfectionist and slave driver. None of John's salespeople could do proposals, presentations, or consultative selling as well as John (at least that is what John thought). For example, he would agonize over each word and sentence in a proposal and would rewrite paragraphs three or four times. John frequently worked 12-14 hour days and pushed his people to the limit.

John learned to play the role of a manager. Unlike Mary in the previous case, he was not afraid to correct employee behavior, deny unrealistic requests, or give low evaluations when warranted. In addition, he held excellent staff meetings and provided clear direction to his people. They always knew what was expected of them. He came across poised and confident to both customers and employees because he always spent a considerable amount of time and energy preparing for individual and group meetings. He rehearsed over and over what he was going to say and carefully planned his response to anticipated questions and objections.

Although John was very good at giving positive feedback (strokes), he was not sincere. He viewed his employees as "things." Since he wasn't concerned about people, he used praise to manipulate his employees to achieve his goals. John also manipulated his boss by forming a close parent-child type of relationship with him. He became successfully dependent on his boss, and his boss became reciprocally dependent on him. John then exploited this dependency to get what he wanted.

John became a master at corporate politics and continued to climb the corporate ladder. He spent two years as regional sales manager and three years as national sales manager. Finally, John was promoted to vice president of marketing.

John often sits in his new executive office trying to figure himself out. He thinks about his moods, examines his motives, and becomes depressed over his loneliness. Sometimes he listens to the ringing in his ears. He can only hear it when he thinks about it. John's extraordinary success in the company hasn't helped his insecurity. He continues to worry about his job performance and is never satisfied with his accomplishments.

John has learned to play the executive role well. However, his personal life is a disaster. He recently experienced his third divorce, has no close friends, and frequently turns to alcohol for comfort. Unlike the corporate world, John feels very shy and awkward in social situations and avoids them like the plague. His corporate role is his suit of armor, and without it he feels naked.

Privately shy managers, like John, often escape detection. They hide their anxiety using well-learned social skills, and avoid situations where they are not in control. The same executive who talks with impressive confidence in the boardroom may blush and become tongue-tied during an introduction at a neighbor's party. Or, they may turn to alcohol to reduce their anxiety and suppress their physical stress reactions. *Privately shy managers can fool some of the people all of the time, and all of the people some of the time, but they can never fool themselves.*

Privately shy people are one of the most fascinating topics in the study of human behavior. Their ability to project poise and confidence in the spotlight baffled many psychologists for years. Many actors, comedians, talk-show hosts, politicians, teachers, and executives are privately shy and only feel comfortable when they are playing a role.

Although privately shy managers may suffer in their personal life, they are obviously better off in the corporate world than publicly shy managers. Most privately shy managers have learned to play the manager role well, and communicate effectively to their superiors, subordinates, and peers. However, their aggressive management style and their manipulative techniques frequently cause employee morale problems.

THE CHRONICALLY SHY MANAGER

Andrew is a 38 year-old accounts payable supervisor for a state government agency. His promotion, five years ago, was largely based on seniority. Andrew supervises eight accounting clerks.

Andrew was labeled shy early in life by his parents, teachers, and friends. He was a highly nervous, self-conscious child. He felt he was too fat, and too ugly, compared to his classmates. Andrew would always sit in the back of the room. He was afraid to ask questions or speak out in class.

In college, Andrew found comfort in numbers and majored in accounting. Although his academic life was manageable, his personal life was a catastrophe. He suffered extreme anxiety in social situations and experienced panic attacks in large crowds. Andrew also failed miserably with the opposite sex and finally gave up on dating. By the end of college his shyness had become progressively worse, and he found himself wanting more and more isolation from people.

Andrew rarely comes out of his office (he even eats lunch there every day), and abdicates much of his supervisory responsibility to Helen, the head clerk. She trains new clerks, monitors workflow, and resolves employee conflicts. Andrew avoids his superiors, peers, and employees whenever possible, and relies heavily on e-mail for communication.

Andrew is fortunate that he works for a state government agency where most of the human contact for new employees is handled by the human resource department. They verify employment history, perform background checks, conduct screening interviews, and administer proficiency exams. The final employment interview, conducted by Andrew, is only a formality and usually lasts only several minutes. As short as it is, it is still very painful for him.

Andrew is required to perform a formal, written evaluation on each of his employees every year. Avoiding any possibility of confrontation, Andrew always writes good evaluations for everyone. He then E-mails the evaluations to his employees and asks them to see him if there are any issues or concerns. There never are!

Andrew never married and lives with his mother four blocks from work. Although he owns a car, he walks to work every day. He rarely drives because traffic makes him extremely nervous. Andrew always eats at home and does most of his shopping on the Internet. He suffers severe anxiety in restaurants, shopping malls, and other places where people gather. Andrew is chronically shy and has sentenced himself to a life of pain, suffering, and isolation.

Employees of chronically shy managers also suffer. They rarely receive the feedback and guidance necessary for their improvement and development. And, they are denied the opportunity to express their ideas and suggestions. This lack of communication causes low morale, high turnover, and ultimately, decreased productivity.

There are very few chronically shy managers in the corporate world. They are usually found in companies and government agencies where seniority is the major factor in determining promotions. For obvious reasons, chronically shy people have a very difficult time assuming management responsibilities.

THE TRANSITIONALLY SHY MANAGER

Susan is 30 years old and the manager of a branch bank. She has always considered herself shy, but has never let her shyness control her life. Although Susan was quiet, soft-spoken, and reserved in high school, she belonged to several social clubs and had several close friends. At first, she was extremely uncomfortable with dating. She would blush and become tongue-tied on first dates. However, once she went out with the same person several times, she would become less shy and more confident in herself.

Susan became a bank teller right out of high school. The first few weeks were very difficult. She would often blush and become tongue-tied when talking to customers and other employees. But, after several weeks on the job, she became more confident and her shyness decreased. Susan was extremely conscientious and became one of the best tellers at the bank.

After four years, Susan was transferred to another branch and promoted to head teller. The new working environment, coupled with supervisory responsibility, made her feel insecure.

Her shyness increased, and her physical stress reactions, like blushing, became more noticeable. At first, Susan's supervisory style was very passive. She wanted her employees to like her, so she rarely corrected employee behavior. Also, she was reluctant to ask employees to do unpleasant tasks and was afraid to deny unrealistic requests. Fortunately, Susan's manager noticed this behavior and spent a considerable amount of time helping her become more assertive. In addition, the bank's corporate headquarters had an excellent training department and offered a comprehensive program for new supervisors. Susan successfully finished the program and eventually became a good supervisor.

During the next few years, Susan went to school at night and completed her college degree in business. Her career at the bank was also progressing quite nicely. First, she was promoted to assistant branch manager, and then, several years later, she was promoted to branch manager. Each time Susan was placed in a new working environment, or given more responsibility, her shyness increased and her physical stress reactions became more pronounced. However, after a short period of time in her new assignment, she would become more confident, and her shyness would decrease.

Susan is a transitionally shy manager. She will always be shy, but she is determined to never let shyness control her life. Transitionally shy managers act and feel shy during certain stages of their career, such as starting a new job, being promoted to a new position, or being transferred to a new location. Other situations that could trigger increased anxiety and shyness include membership on a new committee, or increased responsibility, like a new project. Transitional shyness is a common response to uncertain and unpredictable situations. In these threatening situations, transitionally shy managers display the characteristics of publicly shy managers. But once they adjust to these new circumstances, they become more confident in their abilities, and their shyness decreases.

WHAT CAUSES SHYNESS?

No discussion of shyness would be complete without some examination of cause. While shy characteristics are well defined and universally accepted by most psychologists, *the cause of shyness is not.* Many books and articles have been written on the cause of shyness, and many theories have been presented on this topic. Although a detailed analysis of this subject is beyond the scope of this book, we will briefly examine two of the most widely held theories. Some researchers believe that people are born shy, while others believe that people learn how to become shy. Scientists involved in genetic research believe that shyness is an inherited trait, like the color of your eyes, and therefore runs in families. They have traced genetic links among generations of shy and not-so-shy family members, and tracked the evolution of timidity through various species. On the other hand, behavioral psychologists believe that we are what we have learned and that shy people lack self-esteem. They also believe that shy people have not developed the social skills necessary for successfully relating to others.

Although the genetic research is impressive, I have to agree with Dr. Bernardo Carducci, a behavioral psychologist and leading shyness researcher. He is convinced that people are not born shy. He reminds us that shyness is related to self-consciousness, and children don't become aware of themselves until about age two. *Therefore, infants can't be shy since they don't have a sense of self.* However, Dr. Carducci does point out that some babies are highly reactive. These babies are extremely sensitive to stimulation and become distressed when they feel overwhelmed by unfamiliar people, objects, or situations. Nevertheless, this predisposition to reactivity does not sentence you to a life of social inhibition.

The behavioral psychologists believe that low self-esteem and lack of self-confidence play a major role in shyness. They are convinced that self-esteem and self-confidence are molded by early childhood experiences with parents, teachers, and friends. Some of these experiences involve the kind of feelings children are allowed to express, how they are given attention and recognition, and the way they are labeled or criticized. The behaviorists believe there is no one cause of shyness. Instead, many factors may influence this complex personality trait:

- Emotional and/or physical abuse

- Inconsistent parental discipline

- Critical and/or demanding parents

- Overprotective parents

- Shy parents

- Death of a parent

- Divorced parents

- Frequent moves

- Negative experience with friend(s)

- Negative experience with teacher(s)

Fortunately, the habits acquired in childhood can be replaced with more constructive ones later in life. You can unlearn old behaviors and replace them with new behaviors that will help you become a more effective manager. This requires a comprehensive self-improvement program to change your behavior. You start this journey in the next chapter.

CHAPTER HIGHLIGHTS

• Managerial shyness spans a wide psychological continuum, and can vary from occasional feelings of nervousness to overwhelming anxiety.

• The low range of shyness includes managers who experience mild nervousness such as dry mouth, "butterflies," perspiration, or heart palpitations before an important event.

• The middle range of shyness includes managers who frequently feel intimidated and awkward in certain situations with certain types of people. They are usually shy because they lack self-confidence, social skills, and techniques for managing assertively.

• The high range of shyness includes managers who have an extreme fear of people and are incapacitated by overwhelming anxiety. They stay in their office most of the time and delegate much of their supervisory responsibility to a subordinate.

• Although shyness takes many forms and spans a wide psychological continuum, there are three general characteristics of managerial shyness: silence, physical stress reactions, and self-consciousness.

• Shy managers have a disposition to remain silent. They do not speak up in meetings and are reluctant to correct employee behavior. Many prefer the detachment of e-mail to personal meetings.

• Shy managers frequently exhibit physical stress reactions when placed in uncomfortable situations. These physiological symptoms of anxiety include blushing, trembling, upset stomach, dry mouth, perspiration, clammy hands, faintness, and heart palpitations.

- Shy managers are extremely self-conscious, and are obsessed with the self-analysis of their thoughts and feelings. This characteristic manifests itself in both a public and a private dimension.

- Publicly shy managers are concerned about their awkward behavior and appearance in public. There insecurity and strong need for approval force them to constantly analyze how other people perceive them.

- Privately shy managers are more concerned with feelings than behavior. They are always trying to figure themselves out and are constantly examining their mood, motivation, and sense of worth.

- Chronically shy managers have an extreme fear of people. They avoid social situations and adhere to strict, regimented routines in order to reduce the uncertainty and risk in their daily lives.

- Transitionally shy managers act and feel shy when they are placed in new and uncertain situations. However, once they adjust to these new situations, they become more confident and their shyness decreases.

- While shy characteristics are well defined, the cause of shyness is not. Some researchers believe that people are born shy, while others believe that people learn how to become shy.

- Behavioral psychologists believe that low self-esteem and lack of self-confidence play a major role in shyness. They are convinced that self-esteem and self-confidence are molded by early childhood experiences with parents, teachers, and friends.

PART II
REDUCING
YOUR SHYNESS

3

TAKING CONTROL OF YOUR LIFE

The previous chapters have focused on understanding managerial shyness. Starting with this chapter, the focus will be directed toward you—the shy manager. As a shy manager, you will be confronted with one of the toughest challenges of your life—*the challenge to change your behavior.* Change is painful. Every fiber in your body will resist your attempt to change. This journey will require extraordinary commitment, motivation, and energy.

CHANGING YOUR BEHAVIOR

Don't be fooled by the marketing ads from the pharmaceutical industry. *There is no quick cure for shyness.* Although these medications are being prescribed as a cure for social phobia, do they address the entire problem? While medications may be effective at reducing anxiety levels, Dr. Bernardo Carducci believes a more comprehensive program is required to change the behavior of a shy person. There are no short cuts. Building self-esteem and developing self-confidence are important prerequisites for changing shy behavior. And, what about social skills? There are no pills that will instantly improve your communication techniques and social skills. Medication may be an effective aid in reducing anxiety, but there is no substitute for the long, hard work of unlearning all of the negative thoughts that drive your shy behavior.

In order to change, you first must believe that change is possible, and second, you must really want to change. All of the suggestions and exercises in this book can only be of value if you have made the commitment to change your behavior. You can lead a horse to water, but you can't force it to drink. Likewise, I can lead you to numerous exercises, but I can't force you to do them. Only you can make that commitment.

Change is possible. An enormous body of research exists to support the conclusion that human personality and behavior are quite changeable. Many people have learned how to reduce their shyness, and you can become one of them.

YOU CONTROL YOUR FEELINGS

Without a doubt, the idea that you control your feelings is one of the most important concepts in this book. Although it is the cornerstone for many self-help books, I was first exposed to this idea many years ago in Dr. Wayne Dyer's self-help classic, *Your Erroneous Zones.* Although Dr. Dyer's book doesn't specifically address shyness, many of the concepts in his book can be applied to shyness.

Shy feelings don't happen automatically. They are reactions you *choose* to have. Let's examine the logic:

First, only you alone can control your thoughts. Not your boss. Not your employees. You can choose to have positive thoughts (feeling adequate and confident), or you can choose to have negative thoughts (feeling inadequate and insecure).

Second, it is impossible to have a feeling (emotion) without first having experienced a thought. You must have a signal from your brain to trigger an emotional reaction such as blushing or heart palpitations.

Third, if you control your thoughts, and your feelings come from your thoughts, then you control your feelings. Therefore, if you control your thoughts and feelings, *you have the power to control your shyness.* The conclusion is irrefutable.

The above concept is so simple and obvious, yet so profound. The discovery of this idea marked a turning point in my life. I suffered through 35 years of shyness before I found this revelation. I can honestly say that much of my personal and professional success comes from practicing this concept. I use it every day!

Many of you believe that people make you feel shy. That is not true! You make yourself feel shy because of the thoughts that you have about these people. Once you learn how to change these thoughts, you will have taken a giant step toward reducing your shyness.

Mel, a young supervisor, spends a considerable amount of time worrying because his boss makes him feel insecure. In reality, Mel is the one who makes himself feel insecure because of the thoughts he is having about his boss. Mel's insecurity is actually triggered by his low self-esteem, lack of self-confidence, and his negative thoughts concerning his boss.

We have all grown up in a society that has taught us not to be responsible for our feelings. The following are a few of the messages that you use every day to escape the responsibility for your feelings:

- "Art makes me angry."

- "John hurt my feelings."

- "Presentations make me nervous."

- "Flying frightens me."

- "Susan made me feel stupid."

- "The general manager intimidates me."

- "Linda made a fool of me in the meeting."

Each of these statements carries a subtle message—you are not responsible for your feelings. Let's examine some of these statements in more detail to reinforce this important concept of accepting responsibility for your own feelings. First, "Art makes me angry." How can anyone make you angry? They don't control your feelings. Your boss or employees can say something to you, or take some action concerning you, but they cannot make you angry. You make yourself angry by thinking hostile thoughts about the person or situation. The same reasoning applies to the next statement, "John hurt my feelings." John can't hurt your feelings. Only you can hurt your feelings by thinking negative thoughts about yourself. The third statement demonstrates the fallacy that events control your feelings. Presentations cannot make you nervous. You make yourself nervous by worrying about the presentation. Often, your stress reactions start before you enter the room.

Taking control of your thoughts and feelings begins with *awareness*. You must carefully listen to yourself, and correct yourself, whenever you say things like, "You hurt my feelings." Every time you hear yourself placing responsibility for your feelings on others, an alarm must go off. You have spent years reinforcing thoughts that do not accept responsibility for your feelings. You must now commit the time and energy to new thinking that accepts responsibility for your own feelings.

EXERCISE 3.1

Type the following sentences on several small cards:

I control my thoughts.

My thoughts control my feelings.

Therefore, I control my feelings.

Place these cards where you can see them every day to increase your awareness of this important concept (computer monitor, desk, credenza, wallet, etc.). Review this concept before meetings and presentations. If you begin to think positive thoughts before and during every interpersonal situation, you will be amazed at the outcome.

You must catch yourself every time you hear yourself placing responsibility for your feelings on others. Stop, and correct yourself! Carry a small pad around in your pocket or purse so you can jot down your words. Review your notes every night. At the end of each week review your notes and look for recurring patterns and themes that characterize your self-defeating behavior. Reward yourself for documented progress in accepting responsibility for your feelings. Give yourself a treat. Go to a fine restaurant, a movie, shopping, or some other pleasurable activity. You have earned it.

ROADBLOCKS TO CHANGE

Taking control of your thoughts and feelings will not be easy. Dr. Wayne Dyer points out there are neurotic rewards for hanging on to self-defeating behavior. If you place responsibility for your feelings on others, then they, not you, are responsible for how you feel. Therefore, any change is impossible, since it is their fault that you feel the way you do. This helps you avoid changing. Also, if they are responsible for your feelings, and you can't change, you don't have to take any risks. *Avoiding responsibility, change, and risk are key factors in all self-destructive thinking and behavior.* In simple terms, it is just plain easier and less risky to let others be responsible for your feelings.

Another roadblock to change is *procrastination.* Taking responsibility for procrastination is very different than taking responsibility for feelings. It is very difficult to blame others for your procrastination. You alone are responsible for "putting things off."

Procrastination comes into play when you are faced with a situation that is unpleasant or difficult. You may be afraid that you won't like doing the task, or you may be afraid that you won't do it well. In either case, by telling yourself that you will do the task in the future, you avoid the responsibility of doing the task now. Some examples of procrastination are presented below:

- Postponing your new self-improvement program

- Putting off the evaluation of a problem employee

- Staying in a frustrating job with no chance for advancement

- Postponing the employee meeting on salary issues

- Putting off asking your boss for a raise

- Avoiding disciplinary action on a problem employee

- Delaying a risky decision or project

- Being afraid to bring a problem or bad news to your boss

- Avoiding a confrontation with one of your peers

- Putting off your response to routine correspondence and messages

There are many rewards for putting things off. Here are some of the more important ones:

- You can avoid unpleasant tasks

- You might be able to get someone else to do the task

- You can avoid having to fail by avoiding risky tasks

- You can avoid immediate responsibility and accountability

Rationalization is another powerful roadblock to change. People are remarkably skillful rationalizers. They can find all kinds of ways to justify keeping their self-defeating behaviors. Let's take a look at some of the common rationalizations that shy managers use to justify their behavior:

- "Maybe shyness isn't so bad after all. Shy people are modest and reserved. I don't want to become obnoxious and pretentious."

- "I've been managing people for 20 years, and I've learned that employees respect you more if you keep your distance."

- "I always give my employees the benefit of the doubt. Disciplinary action always creates morale problems. Remember, our legal system is based on the premise that it is better to let ten guilty people go free than to convict one innocent person."

- "So I didn't get the promotion. I can make more money by keeping my non-exempt status and working overtime. Besides, supervising people is a pain in the butt."

- "I always take my time in making decisions. A quick decision is usually a bad decision."

- "These self-improvement courses are a waste of time and money. They make you feel better in the short-run, but in the long-run, everyone knows that people don't change."

- "I just don't have the time to take the class on managing assertively. Why don't we send the employees to class? They are the ones who cause all the problems."

Notice the common theme. Procrastination and rationalization go hand-in-hand. Procrastination allows you to avoid the responsibility of doing things now, and rationalization allows you to feel comfortable with your self-delusional thinking.

SETTING REALISTIC EXPECTATIONS

You are shy. And, realistically, you may always be shy. You can, however, significantly reduce your shyness by taking control of your feelings, building your self-esteem, and developing your self-confidence. In addition, by learning some very important social skills and assertiveness techniques, you can successfully manage your remaining shyness.

You can change much of your shy personality by hard work, but it is practically impossible to totally eliminate your shyness. The amount you reduce your shyness depends on your level of commitment, motivation, and energy. If you religiously practice all of the exercises in this book, you should be able to reduce your shyness by 50%. That is a realistic goal. *And, many of you will exceed it.*

Even if you could, why would you want to totally eliminate all of your shy characteristics? As we pointed out earlier, there are many positive aspects to shyness. Keep the positive traits, and change the ones that interfere with your ability to manage effectively. You alone have the power to change your behavior. A significant reduction in your shyness, coupled with effective assertiveness techniques, may be the edge you need to succeed as a manager.

TAKING THE PLUNGE

My family and I recently went on vacation to Cedar Point, one of the largest amusement parks in the world. My two teenage sons, who are avid roller coaster enthusiasts, wanted to ride Millennium Force, one of the tallest and fastest roller coasters in the world. As we approached the park, I saw Millennium Force's lift hill. It towered a breathtaking 310 feet into the air. I realized at that moment that I could not ride this coaster.

During our first day at the park, I watched my sons ride to the top of Millennium Force's lift hill. Once there, they plummeted to earth at 94 miles per hour, at a staggering 80-degree angle (90-degrees is straight down)! The train then whipped into a high bank turn and started its incredible journey through the park. When they exited the ride, their faces were beaming, and they immediately ask me to join them for a second ride. Fortunately, the line was too long for another ride that day. Unfortunately, the line was short the next morning.

While standing in line the next day, I noticed that 90% of the people waiting were children and teenagers, and the other 10% were adults much younger than I. As I waited in line, and watched the trains climb to the top of the lift hill, anxiety and fear started to take control of my mind and body. When we finally reached the loading area, my knees were trembling and my legs felt like rubber. Every fiber in my body screamed for retreat. Then I looked at my sons and remembered the advice I had given them on numerous occasions. "Don't let your fears control your life." I composed myself, slid into the bucket seat, and fastened the seat belt. The rest is history.

Now it's time for you to overcome your fears, and take control of your life. Shyness revolves around the fear of people. In order for you to become a happier person, and a more effective manager, you must reduce this fear. If you really want to reduce your shyness, you must commit to the self-improvement exercises contained in this book. Simply reading the exercises will not suffice. You must do them. It requires a tremendous amount of hard work to unlearn all the self-defeating thoughts that you have assimilated during your life. Change is not easy, and it does not come fast. If you have realistic expectations, and are persistent in your quest for a better life, I am confident that you will succeed.

CHAPTER HIGHLIGHTS

- Changing behavior is painful. However, an enormous body of research exists to support the conclusion that human personality and behavior are quite changeable.

- You control your thoughts, and your thoughts control your feelings. Therefore, you control your feelings.

- Only you alone can control your thoughts. You can choose to have positive thoughts (feeling adequate and confident), or you can choose to have negative thoughts (feeling inadequate and insecure).

- People do not make you feel shy. You make yourself feel shy because of the thoughts that you have about these people. Once you learn how to change these thoughts, you will reduce your shyness.

- Taking control of your thoughts and feelings begins with awareness. You must listen carefully to yourself, and correct yourself, whenever you hear yourself placing responsibility for your feelings on others.

- There are many roadblocks to change, and avoiding responsibility is a common theme in all of them.

- If you place responsibility for your feelings on others, then they, not you, are responsible for how you feel. Therefore, any change is impossible, since it is their fault that you feel the way you do.

- Procrastination and rationalization are also powerful roadblocks to change. Procrastination allows you to avoid the responsibility of doing things now, and rationalization allows you to feel comfortable with your self-delusional thinking.

- Before you undertake any self-improvement program, it's important to set realistic expectations. You can change much of your shy personality by hard work, but it is practically impossible to totally eliminate your shyness. The amount you reduce your shyness depends on your level of commitment, motivation, and energy.

4

SELF-ASSESSMENT: LOOKING INWARD

How shy are you in interpersonal situations at work? Do you become nervous when you have to correct employee behavior? Are you afraid to ask your employees to do unpleasant tasks? How do you feel when you have to bring "bad news" to your boss? These are the types of questions that you will be asked in this chapter as you begin your process of self-discovery. Honest answers to questions like these reveal important information about the degree of your managerial shyness.

The self-assessment questions and exercises will give you a chance to take a close look at yourself. I'm sure most of you have some preconceived notion about your shyness. However, I doubt many of you have systemically analyzed the type of interpersonal work situations that facilitate your shy reactions or the severity of these reactions. Many of you will learn that you are not as shy as you think you are. And, some of you will discover that your shyness is more prevalent than you thought.

A DOUBLE-EDGED SWORD

Self-assessment is a double-edged sword. As you have already learned, one of the major characteristics of managerial shyness is self-consciousness or preoccupation with self. Self-assessment will initially increase your self-awareness and self-consciousness, making you even more sensitive to your shyness. Why then is this process so important to your self-improvement program?

First, self-assessment will allow you to take an honest look at yourself and accept responsibility for these behaviors. Some of you may be in denial concerning your self-defeating behaviors. You can't change your behavior until you fully accept the responsibility for your behavior. Remember, you alone control your thoughts, feelings, and behavior.

Second, self-assessment will help you objectively measure your managerial shyness. The questions and exercises are designed to help you better understand your problem areas and the severity of your shyness in these areas.

Third, self-assessment will allow you to begin the process of separating yourself from your shyness. Dr. Philip Zimbardo believes that once you get your negative thoughts out of your mind and down on paper, you can then objectively recognize their debilitating nature, and start to distance yourself from them.

Fourth, the initial self-assessment will provide a baseline that can be used to monitor your progress. Look back at these questions after several months to see if your answers have changed. Check back again after six months. Do not check your progress every week. Changing behavior takes time and patience.

During the past several years, hundreds of managers in many diverse industries have taken the Managerial Shyness Survey. The survey has been revised several times based on valuable feedback from psychologists and human relations managers. The following survey is the latest version. The Managerial Shyness Survey can be your first step in coming to grips with your shyness. By answering the questions truthfully, you will begin to understand how shyness affects your professional life.

MANAGERIAL SHYNESS SELF-ASSESSMENT

GENERAL PERCEPTIONS (1-4)

1. How often do you experience shy feelings at work?
    a. Every day
    b. Several times a week
    c. Several times a month
    d. Once a month or less
2. Is your shyness ever a problem for you at work?
    a. Often
    b. Sometimes
    c. Occasionally
    d. Rarely
3. When you are feeling shy at work can you conceal it?
    a. Always
    b. Most of the time
    c. Sometimes
    d. Never
4. What types of people heighten your shyness at work? Circle all that apply.
    a. New subordinate
    b. Aggressive subordinate
    c. Problem subordinate
    d. New peer
    e. Aggressive peer

f. Your manager

g. Aggressive superior

h. All superiors

INTERPERSONAL SITUATIONS – Subordinates (5-18)

Please check how you would feel in each of the following situations.

Not Nervous   Mildly Nervous   Moderately Nervous   Very Nervous

5. Interviewing a prospective new employee _____ _____ _____ _____

6. Delegating work assignments _____ _____ _____ _____

7. Holding employee staff meetings _____ _____ _____ _____

8. Setting expectations and limits for employees _____ _____ _____ _____

9. Correcting employee behavior _____ _____ _____ _____

10. Conducting a formal disciplinary action _____ _____ _____ _____

11. Asking employees to do unpleasant tasks _____ _____ _____ _____

12. Denying unrealistic employee requests _____ _____ _____ _____

13. Conducting employee evaluations _____ _____ _____ _____

14. Conducting a low employee evaluation _____ _____ _____ _____

15. Intervening in employee conflicts _____ _____ _____ _____

16. Employee challenges you in private _____ _____ _____ _____

17. Employee challenges you in public _____ _____ _____ _____

18. Conducting an employee termination _____ _____ _____ _____

INTERPERSONAL SITUATIONS – Superiors (19-33)

Please check how you would feel in each of the following situations.

Not Nervous   Mildly Nervous   Moderately Nervous   Very Nervous

19. Interviewing for a new position _____ _____ _____ _____

20. Asking for a promotion or raise _____ _____ _____ _____

	Not Nervous	Mildly Nervous	Moderately Nervous	Very Nervous
21. Bringing a problem to your boss				
22. Bringing "bad news" to your boss				
23. Asking your boss for time off				
24. Asking your boss for additional resources				
25. Complaining to your boss				
26. Being asked a question by your boss in private and you don't know the answer				
27. Being asked a question by your boss in public and you don't know the answer				
28. Saying "no" to your boss concerning unrealistic assignments or deadlines				
29. Disagreeing with your boss in private				
30. Disagreeing with your boss in public				
31. Being criticized by your boss				
32. Having a confrontation with your boss				
33. Being introduced to someone in top mgt.				

INTERPERSONAL SITUATIONS – Peers & Groups (34-48)

Please check how you would feel in each of the following situations.

	Not Nervous	Mildly Nervous	Moderately Nervous	Very Nervous
34. Bringing a problem to a peer				
35. Asking a peer for information or help				
36. Complaining to a peer				
37. Being asked a question by a peer in private and you don't know the answer				
38. Being asked a question by a peer in public and you don't know the answer				
39. Denying unrealistic peer requests				
40. Disagreeing with a peer in private				

	Not Nervous	Mildly Nervous	Moderately Nervous	Very Nervous
41. Disagreeing with a peer in public	___	___	___	___
42. Being criticized by a peer	___	___	___	___
43. Having a confrontation with a peer	___	___	___	___
44. Speaking to a small group	___	___	___	___
45. Speaking to a large group	___	___	___	___
46. Presenting a proposal to top mgt.	___	___	___	___
47. Asking questions in your manager's staff meetings	___	___	___	___
48. Expressing your views and opinions in your manager's staff meetings	___	___	___	___

STRESS REACTIONS AND SELF-Consciousness (49-60)

49. Check any of the following behaviors that might indicate to others at work that you are feeling shy:

    ___ A reluctance to talk   ___ Talking fast

    ___ Low speaking voice   ___ Stuttering

    ___ Lack of eye contact   ___ Posture

50. Check any of the following stress reactions that you experience with shyness at work:

    ___ Perspiration   ___ Dry mouth

    ___ Upset stomach   ___ Tremors

    ___ Heart pounding   ___ Blushing

    ___ Light-headed   ___ Dizzy

    ___ Fatigue   ___ Other (specify below)

    _____

    _____

51. Review your answers to questions 5 thru 48.
    In which interpersonal situations do you experience the most severe stress reactions? *(Select the top five and order them below starting with the most severe.)*

    Interpersonal Situation   Stress Reaction(s)

    _____   _____

    _____   _____

    _____   _____

    _____   _____

    _____   _____

52. I'm concerned about what my employees think of me.
    a. Strongly agree
    b. Agree
    c. Disagree
    d. Strongly disagree

53. I wish my boss would give me more feedback on my job performance.
    a. Strongly agree
    b. Agree
    c. Disagree
    d. Strongly disagree

54. After I make a presentation, I continue to think about it and critique it in my mind.
    a. Strongly agree
    b. Agree
    c. Disagree
    d. Strongly disagree

55. I'm concerned about my management style.
    a. Strongly agree
    b. Agree
    c. Disagree
    d. Strongly disagree

56. I worry about making a good impression on my boss.
    a. Strongly agree
    b. Agree
    c. Disagree
    d. Strongly disagree

57. I'm concerned about what my peers think of me.
    a.   Strongly agree
    b.   Agree
    c.   Disagree
    d.   Strongly disagree

58. I'm self-conscious about my appearance at work.
    a.   Strongly agree
    b.   Agree
    c.   Disagree
    d.   Strongly disagree

59. After a meeting with my boss, I go back to my office and try to analyze it.
    a.   Strongly agree
    b.   Agree
    c.   Disagree
    d.   Strongly disagree

60. I think about myself a lot.
    a.   Strongly agree
    b.   Agree
    c.   Disagree
    d.   Strongly disagree

DEMOGRAPHIC INFORMATION (61-63)

61. Please indicate your sex:
    _____male   _____female

62. Please check your current level of management:
    _____Supervisory
    _____Middle management
    _____Upper management

62. Please indicate the total number of years experience you have in supervising people:
    _____Years

If you are willing, I would like to add your survey results to our growing body of knowledge about managerial shyness. All information will be kept confidential. Please send survey results to:

Ronald R. Johnson
PO Box 915846
Longwood, FL 32791-5846

EVALUATING YOUR RESPONSES

Now that you have completed your self-assessment, you can evaluate your responses. The first four questions give you an opportunity to acknowledge your shy feelings at work. You can't change your behavior until you fully accept responsibility for your behavior. As you look back on your responses to these questions, remember that shyness spans a wide psychological continuum and can vary from occasional feelings of nervousness to overwhelming anxiety. While some of you experience shy feelings every day, others may experience them only once or twice a month. Don't become discouraged if you indicated that you experience shy feelings "Every day" and these feelings "Often" result in problems for you at work. I applaud your honesty. Recognizing, and accepting, the extent of your managerial shyness is a major step in your self-improvement program.

The next section of the self-assessment required you to measure your level of nervousness in interpersonal situations. The first group of statements describes subordinate situations and reflects routine supervisory functions. If most of your checks were in the "Not Nervous" column, with a few in the "Mildly Nervous" column, your shyness with subordinates is relatively low. Even assertive supervisors may experience some nervousness in serious employee conflicts, challenges, and terminations. However, if many of your checks were in the "Mildly Nervous" and "Moderately Nervous" columns, there is a high probability that your shyness with subordinates is strong enough to adversely impact your job performance. Clearly, if many of your checks were in the "Moderately Nervous" and "Very Nervous" columns, you have a serious shyness problem with subordinates.

The second group of statements outlines interpersonal situations with a superior. These situations are often more threatening than interpersonal situations with a subordinate. If most of your checks were in the "Not Nervous" column, with a few in the "Mildly Nervous" column, your shyness with superiors is relatively low. Even assertive managers can experience some nervousness when they have a confrontation with their boss or interview for a new position. If many of your checks were in the "Mildly Nervous" and "Moderately Nervous" columns, there is a high probability that your shyness with superiors is strong enough to adversely impact your job performance. And, if many of your checks were in the "Moderately Nervous" and "Very Nervous" columns, you have a serious shyness problem with superiors.

The third group of statements describes interpersonal situations with peers and groups. If most of your checks were in the "Not Nervous" column, with a few in the "Mildly Nervous" column, your shyness with peers and groups is relatively low. Even assertive supervisors can experience some nervousness when they speak to a large group or have a confrontation with a peer. If many of your checks were in the "Mildly Nervous" and "Moderately Nervous" columns, there is a high probability that your shyness with peers and/or groups is strong enough to adversely impact your job performance. And, if many of your checks were in the "Moderately Nervous" and "Very Nervous" columns, you have a serious shyness problem with peers and/or groups.

The next three questions give you an opportunity to acknowledge your shy stress reactions at work. Your answer to question 51 is especially important. By identifying the interpersonal situations that trigger your most severe stress reactions, you may discover a common denominator in your managerial shyness.

The last section of the self-assessment deals with self-consciousness, a strong characteristic feature of managerial shyness. Are you excessively preoccupied with yourself? If you checked "Strongly agree" or "Agree" on many of the last nine questions, there is a high probability that you are excessively preoccupied with yourself.

ARE YOU A SHY MANAGER?

How do you determine your score on this self-assessment? Are you shy? How shy are you? Unfortunately, there are no simple answers to these questions. Shyness is a complex and puzzling personality trait. This is not a test that you pass or fail. Nor is there a magic score that labels you as either "shy" or "not shy." *Ultimately, you are the best judge of your shyness.* The objective of self-assessment is to help you acknowledge and understand your shy feelings—not put a label on you. Self-assessment is an important prerequisite to the information and exercises that follow in the remaining chapters.

During my research on managerial shyness, I have discovered that shyness is considered a weakness by many managers, and carries a negative connotation in many organizations. Ironically, some of the same managers who do not consider themselves "shy," react with shy symptoms in many situations. It's unfortunate that these managers don't take the time to better understand shy personality traits and the positive aspects of shyness. Remember, shyness is common, widespread, and universal. The percentage of Americans who now consider themselves shy has increased to nearly 50%. Don't be ashamed of your shy personality traits. You are in good company.

CHAPTER HIGHLIGHTS

- Self-assessment is a double-edged sword. It initially increases your self-awareness and self-consciousness, making you even more sensitive to your shyness.

- Self-assessment is an important part of your self-improvement program. It allows you to take an honest look at yourself and objectively measure your managerial shyness. In addition, it provides a baseline that can be used to monitor your progress.

- Self-assessment also helps you to begin the process of separating yourself from your shyness. Once you get your negative thoughts out of your mind and down on paper, you can then objectively recognize their debilitating nature and start to distance yourself from them.

- The Managerial Shyness Survey is not a test that you pass or fail. Nor is there a magic score that labels you as either "shy" or "not shy." The objective of self-assessment is to help you acknowledge and understand your shy feelings—not put a label on you.

- Shyness is considered a weakness by many managers and carries a negative connotation in many organizations. Ironically, some of the same managers who do not consider themselves "shy" react with shy symptoms in many situations.

- The percentage of Americans who now consider themselves shy has increased to nearly 50%. Don't be ashamed of your shy personality traits. You are in good company.

5

BUILDING YOUR SELF-ESTEEM

Do you tend to put yourself down for your mistakes and shortcomings? Do you reject compliments directed at you? Do you give credit to others when it really belongs to you? Are you concerned about what others think or say about you? If you answered "yes" to any of these questions, you may have a problem with your self-esteem.

SHYNESS AND SELF-ESTEEM

Low self-esteem plays a major role in shyness. Shyness researchers have consistently found a significant correlation between shyness and low self-esteem. When shyness is high, self-esteem is low. And, when self-esteem is high, shyness leaves the picture.

One of the main differences between humans and animals is the awareness of self. Humans have the ability to form an identity and attach a value to it. In other words, humans have the capacity to define who they are, and then decide if they like themselves or not. In short, people with low self-esteem have decided not to like themselves. Self-dislike can take many forms.

Here are some examples of this self-defeating behavior:

- Rejecting compliments directed at you ("I'm not that clever. I found the solution by accident.")

- Giving credit to others when it really belongs to you ("Bob and John did all the work. I just coordinated the effort.")

- Talking yourself out of new opportunities for fear of failure ("I'll never be able to do that. They'll see right through me.")

- Not buying something that you want (You tell yourself that you can't afford it, but you really feel you're not worth it.)

- Rejecting yourself first so you're never caught by surprise ("Joan doesn't like me. She will never put me on the committee.")

- Having your opinions validated by others ("Isn't that right, Ann?" "Just ask Mike, he'll tell you.")

- Complaining about yourself ("I have the worst headache." "I don't feel well." "I am so tired today.")

Sound familiar? The list is endless. While the above examples may appear to be trivial, they nevertheless reveal self-rejection. Every day, people with low self-esteem engage in this putting-yourself-down behavior. What causes this self-defeating behavior? And, when did it all start?

THE ORIGIN OF SELF-ESTEEM

Dr. Matthew McKay, author of the self-help classic, *Self-Esteem*, indicates that parenting techniques during the early years of childhood set the stage for self-esteem. Parents hug and praise their children for acceptable behavior and punish them for dangerous, wrong, or annoying behavior. All children grow up with emotional scars from the punishing events and retain conscious and unconscious memories of all those events that made them feel wrong or bad. These early punishing events are where low self-esteem gets its start, feeding on these "not-OK" feelings. There are several factors that determine the strength of these early not-OK feelings.

First, parents lay the foundation for low self-esteem when they make a child feel *morally wrong*, when the issue is really a matter of taste, poor judgment, or failure to perform a task. In some families, a child is made to feel morally wrong if he or she makes too much noise in the house. Other families make interrupting a parent a sin. Some children are made to feel wrong when they forget to put their toys away. Other children are bad if they cry, bad if they spill their food, or bad if they suck their thumb. Also, when children are made to feel wrong or bad, certain words and phrases carry heavy moral messages. If a child hears that they are bad, lazy, stupid, or sloppy, the event is soon forgotten. But, they are left with a lasting sense of wrongness.

Second, the failure of parents to differentiate between *behavior* and *identity* sends a dangerous message to a child. Let's take the case of a small child playing with a sharp knife in the kitchen. If the parent desperately grabs the knife and hysterically screams, "You're a bad boy!" , the child is getting the message that he and his behavior are not-OK. The parent has attacked both the child's behavior and his worth. However, if the parent calmly takes the knife, and gives the child a strong warning about the dangers of the knife, the child is then receiving a message that he is OK but his behavior is not-OK. Parents who learn how to differentiate between behavior and identity raise children who feel better about themselves and have a healthier self-esteem.

Third, constant *criticism* rapidly erodes a child's self-esteem. The ruse that you are not-OK wasn't learned through occasional criticism. It was learned through repeated criticism. You have to hear "what's wrong with you?" and "can't you do anything right?" many times before the message sinks in. But eventually, you get the point – you're not-OK. Also, if the criticism is accompanied by parental anger or withdrawal, the result can be devastating. Parental anger and withdrawal are one of the scariest things a child can experience. Children can tolerate occasional criticism without serious damage to their self-esteem. But, if the criticism is constantly accompanied by anger or withdrawal, the outcome can be disastrous.

Punishing events are terrifying. A child who is spanked or scolded feels a deep sense of rejection since parents are the source of all physical and emotional sustenance. Although children eventually grow up and leave home, the critical parental voice remains inside them forever. Dr. McKay calls this inner voice the *pathological critic*. The critic takes over where the parents leave off. The critic attacks you, judges you, and undermines your self-worth every day of your life.

Although everyone has a critical inner voice, people with low self-esteem tend to have a more brutal one. The critic has a set of rules describing how you should act and scolds you when you violate them. The critic sets unrealistic standards and punishes you for the smallest mistake. The critic compares you to the achievements and abilities of others and berates you when you fall short. The critic keeps a record of your failures but never reminds you of your successes. This critical inner voice erodes your self-worth every day, but is so shrewd that you never notice its destructive effect.

The goal of this chapter is to help you stop this destructive critic—to stop the judgments, the hurt, and the self-rejection. This will not be an easy task because there are many rewards for listening to the critic.

REWARDS FOR SELF-DENUNCIATION

Why would you choose not to like yourself? Where is the payoff? The benefits, while they may be unhealthy, are nevertheless gratifying. Dr. McKay believes these rewards are the key to understanding why you behave in self-defeating ways. Once you comprehend the "why" of self-dislike, and the maintenance system for retaining it, you can begin to change your self-denouncing ways. Here are several powerful rewards for listening to the critic:

First, the critic helps you gain a lot of pity, attention, and approval from others for constantly putting yourself down. Helen, a special projects coordinator, frequently complained to her coworkers that she was a slow learner and had difficulty completing her projects on time. Her reward was the pity and attention she received from her peers. In fact, several of her coworkers felt so sorry for her that they helped her with her projects.

Second, the critic helps you cope with the fear of failure. Robert, a young supervisor, was contemplating a transfer to another department where the job responsibilities were more challenging. However, he began feeling very nervous at the thought of leaving the security of his old job. His critic came to the rescue. The critic said, "You'll never be able to do it. You haven't got enough experience. You'll be fired." Immobilized by this volley of self-rejecting statements, Robert decided to postpone his transfer request. Immediately his anxiety level decreased, and the critic was reinforced. The critic is very effective in rewarding you with reduced anxiety in situations involving change or risk taking.

Third, the critic helps you deal with the fear of rejection. The critic constantly predicts failure so that you're never caught by surprise. "Your boss will never agree to this change." "The committee will reject your proposal." "Dave will not like your report." By anticipating rejection, failure, or defeat, it doesn't hurt quite so badly when it comes. When the critic does accurately predict rejection, the anticipation helps desensitize you to the pain, and the critic is reinforced to keep on predicting.

Fourth, the critic helps you cope with guilt by providing punishment. The critic will make you pay for your sins, and attack you relentlessly for your lies, greed, and selfishness. And, as the attack progresses, you gradually feel a sense of atonement. If you feel guilty enough, you will eventually be exonerated for your transgressions. The critic is reinforced once more because the damage to your self-worth helps you to overcome, for a while, that terrible feeling of wrongness.

Fifth, the critic helps you avoid taking responsibility for changing your behavior. The critic constantly convinces you that it is just plain easier to stay the way you are. Your payoff is remaining the same.

The above rewards are important elements of your self-denouncing maintenance system. They are the reasons you cling to your current behavior. Armed with these new insights, it's time to take charge of yourself and eliminate this self-defeating behavior.

STOPPING SELF-DENUNCIATION

Taking charge of yourself begins with awareness—awareness of what you say to others and awareness of what you say to yourself. You must catch yourself whenever you make self-denouncing statements like:

- "I'm just a slow learner."
- "I was just lucky, I guess."
- "I could have done much better."
- "I'm really not that smart."
- "John did all the work."
- "Isn't that right, Sue?"

It is equally important to catch your inner voice, the critic, when it attacks your self-esteem. This will not be easy since most shy people are extremely self-conscious. They spend a considerable amount of time thinking about themselves, and analyzing past, present, and future events. You must train your mind to sort through an enormous amount of inner dialog and catch the self-denouncing thoughts like:

- "I'll never be able to do that."
- "Can't I do anything right?"
- "He will never hire me."
- "They will never agree with me."
- "What's wrong with me?"
- "She won't like me."

Does this topic sound familiar? It should. This section re-inforces a very important concept introduced in Chapter 3. *You control your thoughts, and your thoughts control your feelings.* If you choose to think negative thoughts about yourself, you will feel insecure and inadequate. If you choose to think positive thoughts about yourself, you will start to feel your self-esteem grow.

EXERCISE 5.1

You must catch yourself every time you make self-denouncing statements or have self-denouncing thoughts. Stop, and correct yourself! Carry a small pad around in your pocket or purse so you can jot down your words or thoughts.

Every night review your notes. On a piece of binder paper, draw a line down the middle. On the left side put the heading, *Self-Denouncing Statement or Thought.* On the right side put the heading, *Reward.* Now, for each self-denouncing statement or thought in your notebook, write down your reward for this behavior.

At the end of each week review your notebook and look for *recurring patterns and themes* that character-ize your self-denouncing behavior. You may discover re-wards of reduced anxiety in situations involving change or risk taking. Or, you may find feelings of atonement if the guilt is strong enough. Whatever the case, once you understand the "why" of your self-denouncing ways, you can begin to change this self-defeating behavior. Reward yourself for documented progress in reducing your self-denunciation.

ELIMINATING YOUR NEED FOR APPROVAL

Approval-seeking is another self-defeating behavior that erodes your self-esteem. Eliminating your need for approval is a central theme in Dr. Wayne Dyer's self-help classic, *Your Erroneous Zones*. Dr. Dyer indicates that wanting approval is healthy, but needing approval is another story. It feels good when we are appreciated for our accomplishments. We all enjoy applause, cheers, kudos, and praise. Approval in itself is not unhealthy. In fact, acceptance is an important measure of our success at all stages of our life. However, when you *seek* approval, you cripple your self-esteem by making others' opinions of you more important than your own self-assessments.

If you want approval, you are simply happy to be accepted by other people. But, if you need approval, and don't get it, frustration and depression take over. When approval-seeking becomes a need, you give up a part of yourself to another person whose advocacy you must have. You have chosen to delegate your self-worth to someone else to accept, or reject, as they see fit. Some examples of approval-seeking behavior are outlined below:

- Asking your boss for permission even when you have full authority to act without it

- Being afraid to ask employees to do unpleasant tasks for fear they won't like you

- Changing your mind in a meeting because your boss, or a peer, shows signs of disapproval

- Being afraid to correct employee behavior for fear they won't like you

- Sugar-coating a statement to avoid an adverse reaction

- Apologizing for yourself so others can forgive you, and approve of you

- Being intimidated by a salesperson and buying something you don't want

- Concurring with a position or proposal even when you don't agree with it

- Being afraid to correct a colleague even when you know they are wrong

- Spreading bad news and enjoying the feeling of being noticed

- Complimenting someone in order to make them like you

Eliminating your need for approval will not be easy. Dr. Dyer points out there are rewards for approval-seeking behavior. These rewards are strikingly similar to the payoffs for not taking control of your thoughts and feelings. They are centered around a familiar theme, placing responsibility for your feelings on others. If you feel hurt or depressed because someone else doesn't approve of you, then they, not you, are responsible for how you feel. And, if they are responsible, then any change in you is impossible, since it is their fault that you feel the way you do. Therefore, as long as they are responsible, and you can't change, you don't have to take any risks. *Once again, avoiding responsibility, change, and risk are key factors in this self-defeating behavior.*

How can you stop this addictive need for approval? Here are some specific strategies for eliminating approval-seeking behavior as a need:

- Stop feeling hurt or depressed because someone didn't approve of you. Accept the fact that many people will never understand you. And, you will never understand them.

- Think positive thoughts when you encounter disapproval. Remember, no one can reject you and hurt your feelings. Only you can do that by thinking negative thoughts.

- Start responding to disapproval with the word "you". For example, when a colleague doesn't agree with you, and is getting angry, simply respond with, "You're getting upset because you feel that I shouldn't think this way." This will reinforce the fact that disapproval belongs to him or her, not you.

- Quit checking out decisions with someone whose opinion you value more than your own. You must start to trust yourself when making routine decisions for which you have full authority.

- Stop having your opinions validated by others with sentences like, "Isn't that right, John?" or "Just ask Sue; she'll tell you."

- Halt passive conversations. If the other person does most of the talking, you are into approval-seeking. Spend more time making statements and less time asking questions and seeking permission.

In addition to the above strategies, it is also important to maintain financial security. There is a close relationship between financial insecurity and approval-seeking behavior at work. If you live from paycheck to paycheck, you may feel insecure at work and find yourself extremely dependent on your employer. On the other hand, if you manage your money wisely, and have sufficient savings, you probably feel more independent and can afford to be more assertive with your boss and coworkers.

For all the reasons discussed in this section, you must make a commitment to eliminate approval-seeking in your life. Do not strive to wipe out all approval; instead, work toward not being immobilized when you don't get the adulations you covet. Applause is gratifying, and approval is a wonderful experience. What you should seek is immunity from pain when you don't get the applause. This will not be an easy task, since you have been conditioned to need approval from your first day on this earth. Eliminating this self-defeating behavior is an important prerequisite to developing a healthier self-esteem.

LEARNING TO LIKE YOURSELF

You cannot reduce your shyness until you increase your self-esteem. And, you cannot increase your self-esteem until you learn to like yourself. It's that simple! Before we embark on this critical journey, you must abandon the idea that you have only one self-image to like or dislike. In actuality, you have many self-images. For example, you have feelings about yourself physically, intellectually, and socially. You have opinions about your abilities in athletics, problem solving, public speaking, and in many other areas too numerous to mention. In order to increase your self-esteem, you must break down your areas of dislike into specifics and work hard on improving each of these self-images.

One area to look at first is your body. Take a real close look. Do you like what you see? Do you like your hair, ears, eyes, nose, cheeks, mouth, and teeth? How about your arms, chest, stomach, waist, buttocks, hips, thighs, and legs? What parts do you dislike? Make sure these are parts that you dislike—not someone else. Never let others dictate your appearance. If these parts can be changed—change them! Don't let procrastination rob you of feeling better about your physical appearance.

Some of these changes are relatively simple. If you don't like your glasses, change the style, or switch to contact lenses. With laser vision correction, you might be able to eliminate the need for glasses or contacts altogether. If you don't like your hair, change the style or color. Or, if hair loss is a major issue, hair restoration clinics offer a variety of surgical and non-surgical procedures. If you don't like your teeth, consult an orthodontist or a dentist specializing in cosmetic dentistry.

Other physical changes are more difficult, and require more effort and determination. If you think you're too thin, then gain weight. If you feel you're overweight, then lose weight. Shape your body the way *you* want. Although proper diet and exercise are important, many research studies have confirmed that a change in lifestyle is essential to long term weight adjustment and maintenance. You must change your eating and exercise habits, and make your body a top priority in your life.

If you can't achieve your objectives through proper diet and exercise, you may want to explore cosmetic surgery. Procedures available include liposuction, abdominoplasty, breast enhancement, rhinoplasty, face and neck lifts, lip enhancement, chin and ear reshaping, and many others too numerous to mention. Some of these procedures are very uncomfortable and expensive, so you need to take a close look at yourself. Are you really that unhappy with your physical appearance? Will these changes improve your self-esteem? Can you learn to live with your current appearance and be happy? If you're concerned about the expense, scrutinize your budget and examine your priorities. Don't short-change your self-esteem. If *you* really want cosmetic surgery, then do it! *You're worth it.*

What about those features that you dislike which cannot

be changed (too tall, too short, etc.)? And, what about those features that you just can't afford to change? You must learn to accept these features and declare them as worthy and attractive to you. *Don't dwell on things you can't change. Instead, focus on the things you can change.*

Now, what do you think about your intelligence? Do you feel that you are less intelligent than others? This may astonish you, but Dr. Wayne Dyer believes that *you can choose to be as intelligent as you desire.* He points out that aptitude is a function of time. With enough time and effort you can master almost any skill. Intelligence is defined as the capacity to acquire and apply knowledge. Do you see a time limit in this definition, or a requirement to master molecular biology or nuclear physics? Of course not. There are many skills that you have chosen not to master, simply because you are not interested in them. That does not make you less intelligent.

If there are areas that interest you, but you feel deficient, then take the time and make an effort to master them. Take that night class in psychology, and increase your knowledge of human behavior. Sign up for that investment seminar, and learn how to make better financial decisions. Or, start on that advanced degree that you've been talking about for the past five years. Stop complaining about your intelligence, and stop procrastinating about improving your deficiencies. *You are as intelligent as you choose to be.* Learning should be a lifelong journey. When you stop learning, you start dying.

It's possible to make the same kind of choices for other self-images. Your athletic, social, artistic, musical, mechanical, and other abilities are largely the result of past choices and priorities. You have the power to change any of these self-images. If you love tennis, but constantly criticize yourself, then take lessons. If you label yourself as incompetent in home repair, then go to a home improvement store and sign up for a workshop.

And finally, you must stop equating your abilities with your own self-worth. *Your worth is determined by you and has nothing to do with your behavior.* You must choose to be worthy to yourself forever, and then get on with the task of improving your self-images. Learning to like yourself will be an incredible journey. It will open doors that have been closed since childhood. It will revitalize you and allow you to live each day to its fullest. It is, without a doubt, the most important prerequisite to improving your self-esteem and reducing your shyness.

You have the power to stop self-denunciation. You have the power to shed your need for approval. And, you have the power to like yourself better. Yes, you have the power to control your thoughts and change your behavior. It is your choice. Today can be the beginning of a new you.

EXERCISE 5.2

It's important to feel good about yourself mentally and physically. A prerequisite to a healthy mind is a healthy body. Make a commitment today to start treating your body better. Select good nutritional foods, eliminate excess weight, and exercise daily. If you have difficulty managing your own fitness program, then join a health club. They have nutritional consultants, personal trainers, running tracks, cardiovascular equipment, free weights, and many other amenities to help you maintain a healthy body. Don't let cost inhibit you from this important task. You're worth it.

Want to feel better about yourself? Then go shopping for some new clothes and accessories. Break out of your normal routine and take a few risks. Try some new specialty stores and look at different styles and colors.

Don't be too practical – make sure you buy some "interesting and creative" clothes. And, indulge yourself with some good designer labels because you're worth it.

Go to a fine restaurant and order an item that you really savor, regardless of the price. Don't forget to order an excellent wine. Also, the next time you go to the grocery store, start selecting items based on want, not price. Your self-denial must become a thing of the past.

Buy a season ticket to an activity that you really enjoy. This could be a sporting activity like basketball or football, or a cultural activity such as the symphony or live theater. In any case, give yourself this special treat because you're worth it.

CHAPTER HIGHLIGHTS

- Low self-esteem plays a major role in shyness. Shyness researchers have consistently found a significant correlation between shyness and low self-esteem.

- Parenting techniques during the early years of childhood set the stage for self-esteem. Low self-esteem can be traced to early punishing events.

- Parents lay the foundation for low self-esteem when they (1) make a child feel morally wrong, (2) fail to differentiate between behavior and identity, and (3) use constant criticism.

- Although children eventually grow up and leave home, the critical parental voice remains inside them forever. This critic takes over where the parents leave off.

- Although everyone has a critical inner voice, people with low self-esteem tend to have a more brutal one.

- There are several powerful rewards for listening to the critic and maintaining self-denunciation. The critic helps you (1) gain a lot of pity, attention, and approval from others, (2) cope with the fear of failure, (3) deal with the fear of rejection, (4) cope with guilt by providing punishment, and (5) avoid taking responsibility for changing your behavior.

- Stopping self-denunciation begins with awareness—awareness of what you say to others and awareness of what you say to yourself. You must catch yourself whenever you have self-denouncing thoughts or make self-denouncing statements.

- Approval-seeking is another self-defeating behavior that erodes your self-esteem. Wanting approval is healthy, but needing approval is another story. When you seek approval, you cripple your self-esteem by making others' opinions of you more important than your own self-assessments.

- The neurotic rewards for approval-seeking behavior are strikingly similar to the payoffs for not taking control of your thoughts and feelings. Once again, avoiding responsibility, change, and risk are key factors in this self-defeating behavior.

- You cannot reduce your shyness until you increase your self-esteem. And, you cannot increase your self-esteem until you learn how to like yourself.

- In actuality, you have many self-images (physical, intellectual, social, etc.) to like or dislike. In order to increase your self-esteem, you must break down your areas of dislike into specifics, and work hard on improving each of these self-images.

- If there are features that you don't like about your body, then change them. Make sure these are features that you dislike, not someone else. If some features can't be changed, you must learn to accept them and declare them as worthy and attractive to you.

- You can choose to be as intelligent as you desire. Aptitude is a function of time. With enough time and effort you can master almost any skill.

- It's possible to make the same kind of choices for other self-images. Your athletic, social, artistic, musical, mechanical, and other abilities are largely the result of past choices and priorities. You have the power to change any of these self-images.

- And finally, you must stop equating your abilities with your own self-worth. Your worth is determined by you and has nothing to do with your behavior. You must choose to be worthy to yourself forever, and then get on with the task of improving your self-images.

6

DEVELOPING YOUR SELF-CONFIDENCE

Self-confidence is an extension of self-esteem. While self-esteem centers on self-worth, *self-confidence deals with the ability to make decisions and take risks.* If you feel good about your decision-making ability, you'll be able to take risks because you are optimistic about the outcome. On the other hand, if you doubt yourself, you will be reluctant to take risks because you are pessimistic about the outcome.

Managers with self-confidence are decisive, action-oriented individuals who confront and solve problems instead of worrying about them. In contrast, managers who lack self-confidence are indecisive and doubt their ability to make decisions or solve problems. They are afraid to take risks and often allow others to make decisions for them. Managers who lack self-confidence are often:

- Afraid to speak up in meetings

- Hesitant to propose new ideas or plans

- Reluctant to change procedures or try new ones

- Inclined to ignore problems in
  hopes they will go away

- Prone to ask permission when it isn't necessary
- Afraid to express views and opinions
- Hesitant to give assignments

THE ORIGIN OF SELF-CONFIDENCE

Self-confidence starts in childhood. If your parents gave you the freedom and autonomy to take risks, you began to develop self-confidence at an early age. On the other hand, if your parents were overprotective and sheltered you from new experiences and risks, your self-confidence never had an opportunity to grow.

When Tim was five, his parents taught him how to skate and ride a bicycle. They also enrolled him in swimming classes and showed him how to water-ski. Tim's father also devoted several hours a week helping Tim learn baseball. In elementary school, Tim's parents encouraged him to participate in school activities. As a result, he was active in student government, school clubs, and sports.

As Tim grew older, and demonstrated responsibility, his parents continued to give him the freedom to explore new things and take risks. His father taught him how to use power tools so he could assist in home improvement projects and lawn maintenance. At age 13, his parents enrolled him in a SCUBA course so he could become a certified diver. In high school, Tim continued to be active in student government, school clubs, and sports. He lettered in swimming and baseball. Tim's parents did an excellent job of giving him the freedom and autonomy to experience new activities, take risks, and build self-confidence.

In contrast, Bill's parents were overprotective during his childhood. Although Bill wanted a bicycle when he was five, his parents waited until he was eight. They felt he was too young to control a bicycle, and would fall and hurt himself. When he finally did get his bicycle he was only allowed to ride it near his home. He was not allowed to ride it to school or outside his neighborhood. Bill's parents were also very concerned about sports injuries. Although they allowed him to play baseball and soccer, they constantly told him to be careful and often warned him about the danger of getting hit with the ball (consequently, Bill developed a fear of the ball). Bill was never allowed to play football because his parents felt there was too much contact. As a result of his parents' overprotection, Bill seemed to struggle in sports and never developed confidence. He was frequently made fun of by other boys and was always chosen last when a group was divided into teams.

Bill's parents were also overprotective in other areas. Bill was not allowed to play with electric trains for fear of being shocked. He was not allowed to use power tools. He was not allowed to climb ladders. He was not allowed to ride roller coasters. The list goes on and on. It's quite obvious that Bill's parents did not give him the opportunity to explore, take risks, and build self-confidence.

Children cannot develop self-confidence without taking risks. However, responsible parents expose their children to *controlled* risks. They *prepare* their children for new experiences and *supervise* them during these experiences. For example, when Tim's parents taught him how to ride a bicycle, they started him with training wheels. After many successful rides, they took the training wheels off, and prepared him for a possible fall. They made sure he was wearing protective clothing, wrist and elbow pads, kneepads, and a helmet. And most important, when Tim did fall, they were right there to pick him up and encourage him to try again.

Teachers also play a crucial role in the development of self-confidence. Effective teachers give positive reinforcement to children who take risks and explore new approaches to assignments and problems. They help children build confidence in classroom discussions, group projects, and presentations. Teachers also help children develop self-confidence in relationships. They show them how to trust each other and share their space, materials, and equipment.

Children need security in their environment, and confidence in their relationships, in order to grow and develop. Security and confidence come from living in an environment with order and predictability, and the freedom and flexibility to experiment, explore, and cope with new and unfamiliar situations. Warm and understanding parents, as well as teachers, play a key role in this process.

Unfortunately, your parents and teachers may not have given you the freedom and autonomy to explore, take risks, and develop self-confidence. As a result, you may have developed into a person who is indecisive and reluctant to make decisions or solve problems. Don't despair—it's not too late to change your behavior. The next section will start you on your journey toward a more confident you.

LEARNING HOW TO TAKE RISKS

You cannot develop your self-confidence until you learn how to take risks. There are many types of risks. First, there are *physical risks*, like breaking a leg in a skiing accident or rupturing your eardrum on a SCUBA dive. Then, there are *psychological risks*, such as being turned down for a date or having your plan rejected at work. Also, there are *financial risks*, like making bad investments or overextending your credit. All of these examples have something in common. They all involve decision-making and fear of failure. So, how do you develop self-confidence and learn how to take risks?

First, you must believe that change is possible and that you can learn how to take risks. Paying lip service to change is not acceptable. You must truly believe that change is possible, but most important, that it is possible for you. A large amount of research exists to support the conclusion that human personality and behavior are quite changeable. Many people have learned how to develop their self-confidence, and you can become one of them.

Second, you must believe in the power of your own mind. You must believe in the power of positive thinking. You control your thoughts. And, your feelings come from your thoughts. Therefore, you control your feelings. People and situations do not make you feel insecure. You make yourself feel insecure because of the thoughts that you have about the people or situations. Once you learn how to change these thoughts, you will experience a significant improvement in your self-confidence.

Third, you must be committed to improving your self-confidence. You must be willing to commit time and energy to this important objective and risk some short-term failures. Every fiber in your body will resist your attempt to change. Do not give in to this resistance. The long-term benefits far outweigh the short-term rewards for keeping these self-defeating behaviors.

Fourth, you must decide what you want to accomplish. In order to improve your self-confidence, you must set specific and realistic goals. Becoming the keynote speaker at the annual international computer exposition is not a realistic goal. Being able to speak up in a staff meeting without physical stress reactions is. Start with small goals, and then work your way up to more difficult ones. How do you eat an elephant? One bite at a time!

Choose one of your goals and break it down into smaller tasks. What needs to be done first? What second? And so forth. Make an outline so you can check off each task as you accomplish it. For example, if you want to speak up in staff meetings,

decide exactly what you want to say. Write it down and practice it. Also, anticipate the questions you might be asked. Write
them down and prepare responses. Reward yourself after successfully completing each task. Give yourself a big reward when
you accomplish your entire goal. You have earned it, and most
important of all, you are worth it. Enjoy the feeling of accom-
plishment.

Now, turn your attention to your next goal, break it down
into smaller tasks, and start working on it. Anything you want
to do in your life can be broken down into smaller parts and accomplished bit-by-bit—just like eating an elephant.

Fifth, you must have patience. Rome wasn't built in a day.
You can't eliminate years of self-defeating behavior in a few
weeks. The key to building self-confidence is to develop small,
realistic goals, and then successfully accomplishing them. *Success reinforces success.* When you have successfully completed
a series of small, low-risk goals, you can then establish more
complex goals with higher levels of risk.

SELF-CONFIDENCE IN YOUR PERSONAL LIFE

One of the main objectives of this chapter is to help you
build self-confidence in both your personal life and your professional life. This section will concentrate on your personal life.
The next section will focus on your professional life. You will
soon discover that developing personal self-confidence will help
you build professional self-confidence.

There are many activities that you can use to develop personal self-confidence. Sports are a traditional favorite. There are
a wide variety of sports activities available, some more risky
than others. Also, many of these activities will help you improve
your body, so you can build your self-esteem at the same time

you are developing your self-confidence.

SCUBA diving is an excellent sport for developing self-confidence. Although exploring the underwater world can be an exhilarating experience, there are many risks associated with this sport. If you descend or ascend too fast, without following the proper procedures for pressure equalization and decompression, you may seriously injure your body. Also, panic as a result of equipment malfunction may result in death. In addition, there are some forms of sea life that many people perceive as dangerous. They include sharks, barracudas, eels, and poisonous sea urchins. However, with proper equipment, and instruction, recreational SCUBA diving is a safe sport.

I have chosen SCUBA diving for the first example because it has all the characteristics of an excellent confidence builder:

- Risk is moderate

- Risk is supervised

- Goal is broken down into smaller tasks

- Immediate reinforcement for achieving tasks

- Subsequent tasks involve more risk

- Opportunity for continuing development

First, SCUBA diving has a moderate degree of risk. It is more challenging than tennis or racket ball, but not as extreme as sky diving or mountain climbing. You have to work hard and take moderate risks to become a certified diver. When you finally receive your certification card, you really feel good about yourself. You have demonstrated your self-confidence.

Second, the risks are supervised. A certified instructor closely supervises all instruction, including breathing techniques, descent and ascent procedures, and simulated equipment malfunctions. The instructor is right next to you from the time you take your first SCUBA breath in a swimming pool until you successfully complete your final open water dive.

Third, SCUBA diving is learned by successfully completing many related tasks and skills. After several classroom sessions, you must pass a comprehensive written exam on SCUBA equipment, techniques, and safety procedures. Also, you must pass surface and underwater endurance swimming tests. And, there are numerous skills you must master before you become certified. Several of the most important ones are listed below:

- Configuring and adjusting SCUBA equipment
- Learning underwater kicking techniques
- Mastering SCUBA breathing techniques
- Clearing a mask and regulator
- Learning buoyancy compensator techniques
- Equalizing ear pressure
- Applying decompression rules and techniques
- Recovering from equipment malfunctions
- Learning buddy breathing techniques
- Mastering emergency ascent procedures

Fourth, you receive immediate feedback after attempting each skill. If successful, the instructor will congratulate you, check you "complete" on the skill list, and start you on the next required skill. If unsuccessful, the instructor will work with you until you successfully complete the skill.

Fifth, subsequent skills involve more risk. For example, learning how to safely descend and ascent involves more risk than learning how to clear water out of a mask and regulator. Emergency ascents are more risky than buddy breathing. And, open water checkout dives are more risky than swimming pool dives.

Sixth, SCUBA diving provides the opportunity for continuing development of self-confidence. There are many excellent dive locations throughout the world, each offering new adventures and challenges. You can easily change the location and complexity of your dives. You can also increase the depth and duration of your dives. In addition, you can enroll in courses for advanced certification in many areas such as cave diving, wreck diving, and search and recovery diving. All these options give you the opportunity to experience challenging new dives, take controlled risks, and build your self-confidence.

Snow skiing is another great sport for developing self-confidence. Like SCUBA diving, it also has all the characteristics of an excellent confidence builder. First, it involves a moderate degree of risk. If you fall the wrong way, you can sprain an ankle or break a leg. If you collide with another person, or a tree, you can seriously injure your body. And, if you don't wear proper clothing, you can develop hypothermia and/or frost bite.

Snow skiing is usually taught by a certified instructor and is learned by successfully completing many related tasks and skills. Some of the more important ones are listed below:

- Configuring and adjusting equipment

- Learning safety procedures

- Using beginning snowplow techniques

- Shifting your weight for control

- Learning how to fall

- Recovering from falls

- Getting on and off rope and T-bar tows

- Getting on and off chair lifts

- Using advanced parallel techniques

The advanced tasks and skills involve more risk than the beginning ones. For example, learning how to get on and off a chair lift is more difficult than learning how to use a rope or T-bar tow. Parallel skiing is more difficult than snowplowing. And, skiing down an advanced slope is definitely more risky than skiing down a beginning or intermediate slope.

Snow skiing also allows for continuing development of self-confidence. There are many excellent ski resorts throughout the world. You can easily change the location and level of difficulty for greater challenges. Like SCUBA diving, snow skiing definitely offers you the opportunity to experience new adventures, take controlled risks, and build your self-confidence.

In addition to SCUBA diving and snow skiing, there are many other sports available for building self-confidence. Team sports include baseball, basketball, football, volleyball, ice hockey, and soccer. Although all of these sports have professional teams, there are many amateur associations that promote and sponsor these sports. Some common individual sports include golf, tennis, racquetball, squash, swimming, springboard diving, track and field, and gymnastics. If you want to push the envelope, there are many other sports available that offer extreme risks. They include auto racing, motorcycle racing, boat racing, snowmobile racing, mountain climbing, and skydiving.

While sports activities usually involve physical risks, other activities may involve psychological or financial risks. The following examples cover a wide range of confidence building activities. Hopefully, some of them will spark your interest.

- Join a volunteer community theater. Start with set construction and work your way up to small speaking parts. You may also want to take an acting class at a local community college to help you prepare for this new adventure.

- Take some money out of that secure savings account and make some intelligent investments. Take advantage of self-help books and investment seminars. Start with small amounts and look for low risk investments. Remember, success reinforces success. Once you gain confidence in your decision-making, you can increase the amount of your investment and the level of risk.

- Stop looking at those roller coasters and start riding them. They won't kill you. Start with the smaller, junior coasters and work your way up to the larger, looping ones. Riding roller coasters is an excellent, controlled risk activity. They scare the pants off you, but make you feel alive.

- Contact your local Sheriff's Office and find out the procedure for becoming a reserve Deputy Sheriff. Most law enforcement academies offer evening and weekend classes. Although you won't get paid for this volunteer work, responding to 911 calls will definitely build your self-confidence.

- Take flying lessons and become a licensed pilot. Contact a local flight school and request information, as well as an introductory flight. Learning how to fly an airplane is an outstanding confidence builder.

- Take sailing lessons and learn how to navigate and sail. Start with small sailboats and work your way up to larger ones. Get your friends together, plan a trip, and rent a large sailboat.

Miami to the Bahamas sounds great.

- Start your own business. To minimize the risk, you may want to operate it part-time in the beginning. Make sure you take advantage of self-help books and small business seminars. A successful small business can be very rewarding.

- Write that book you've been talking about for several years. Take a class in creative writing to help you polish your skills. To get started, you may want to write some articles or short stories for periodicals. This will give you faster feedback on your material and skills. Don't let those initial rejection notices discourage you. If your desire to write and publish is strong enough, you will succeed.

- Become more active in social clubs and organizations. Seek leadership responsibility. Run for an office or volunteer to chair a committee.

- Run for public office. There are numerous full-time and part-time elected positions available in city and county government. Before you run for office make sure you become active in your local political party. You will need their support to run a successful campaign. Networking is everything in politics.

EXERCISE 6.1

Select several goals to develop self-confidence in your personal life. You can use some of the above activities or select others that interest you. Using the methodology discussed in this chapter, take the first goal and break it down into smaller tasks or skills. Reward yourself after successfully completing each task. Give yourself a big reward after successfully completing the entire goal. Follow the same procedure for your other goals.

SELF-CONFIDENCE IN YOUR PROFESSIONAL LIFE

How do you develop self-confidence in business decisions? The same way you develop self-confidence in your personal life. You must learn how to take risks. There is, however, one important difference. While risk-taking in your personal life may result in a sprained ankle or bruised ego, risk-taking in your professional life may result in ostracism, reprimand, demotion, or even termination. Nevertheless, you cannot develop self-confidence in your business decisions until you learn how to take risks.

Knowing *where* and *how* to take risks is one of the most important skills in management. Each time you make a plan, state your opinion, suggest a course of action, or make a decision, you are taking a risk. The plan may not work, your opinion may be rejected, or the decision may be incorrect. Managers who lack self-confidence rarely propose new ideas. They prefer to sit quietly in staff meetings and "be seen but not heard." They also doubt their ability to solve problems. Many ignore a problem as long as possible and procrastinate until the problem escalates into a crisis. Other managers simply abdicate their responsibility and allow other managers or subordinates to make decisions for them.

Learning how to take risks in business is very similar to learning how to take risks in your personal life. You must determine the areas in which you lack self-confidence, and then develop specific goals to address them. Once a goal is identified, it must be broken down into smaller parts or manageable tasks.

Barry is a 28 year-old manager at a boat manufacturing company. Barry joined the company right out of college and has learned a great deal about the business during the past six years. The company is family owned, and upper management is very conservative. They have traditionally built low-priced, 16' to 24' boats that lack custom features, like carpeting and upholstered seats. These boats are primarily used for fishing, as opposed to pleasure boat activities like cruising or water skiing. Barry has recently started to question this strategy and believes the company should add another product line that offers more custom features. Unfortunately, Barry lacks the self-confidence to propose his idea to upper management. The idea may be rejected; or if accepted, the new product line may not be successful. Is there a way to minimize the risk in proposing this new idea? The answer is yes, if Barry follows the tasks outlined below.

First, limit the scope of the idea. To build self-confidence, Barry should take small steps. Remember, success reinforces success. Rather than propose a whole new product line of custom boats, Barry should take one of the current models and propose the addition of some custom features. This will reduce the impact on development and manufacturing operations and minimize the risk of the proposal. If the initial proposal is accepted, and the new product is successful, Barry can then propose additional product enhancements. Also, it is very important from the start for Barry to write down his ideas. Don't worry about formality and organization—just get the ideas down on paper.

Second, perform market research. Barry needs to research the feasibility of his idea. He should take a close look at the competition and the products they offer. In addition, he must analyze the market area and estimate the demand for the proposed product. And finally, he should talk to boat retailers that sell the current product line and get their feedback on product specifications and pricing. If the results of this preliminary analysis look encouraging, it's time to get others involved in the idea.

Barry should first discuss the idea with his manager. Good managers encourage initiative, particularly innovative ideas that could enhance the business. He should also hold some brainstorming sessions with his peers and subordinates. They can help him refine his ideas. A word of caution! When he talks to his boss, he must be careful not to "over sell" the idea at this early stage. If he does, his boss may kill the idea prematurely. Instead, he should give his boss some positive feedback on the preliminary analysis, and tell him that he will keep him informed on the progress of the research. Also, Barry must write down all the information he has obtained during this phase of the research.

Third, develop a preliminary business plan. There are many books and seminars available to help Barry with this process. The preliminary plan should include product specifications, estimated development, manufacturing, and marketing costs, projected sales, and return on investment. Research results and assumptions should also be included in the plan. The decision to limit the scope of the idea should greatly reduce the development and manufacturing costs. While Barry is developing the plan, he should continue to get input from his peers and subordinates, and keep his boss up to date.

It's now time for Barry to take a calculated risk. He must present the plan to his manager. If his boss likes the idea, he will help Barry refine the plan and assist him in selling upper management. Upper management may reject the proposal. Or, if accepted, the new product may not be successful. Although the risk of failure is always present, Barry has taken several important steps to *minimize* this risk. First, he has limited the scope of the idea. Second, he has performed market research and cost analysis on the proposed product. And third, he has practiced *participative management* in refining the idea and developing the business plan. *Research, planning, and participative man-*

agement are essential to minimizing risk in business decision-making.

The above case study outlines the tasks necessary to develop a new product proposal. Let's summarize the steps for *minimizing risk* in proposing new ideas in general:

1. *Limit the scope of the proposal.* Whether it's adding new products or services, expanding sales areas, or increasing automation, limiting the scope of the initial proposal will reduce the risk.

2. *Research the feasibility of your idea.* Is there a demand for the new product or service? Are the demographics of the new sales area compatible with the current products and services? Is the technology really there to support the automation proposal?

3. *Get others involved in the idea if the results of the feasibility analysis look encouraging.* Introduce your manager to the concept, and hold brainstorming sessions with your peers and subordinates. Participative management will help you refine the idea and reduce the risk of the proposal.

4. *Quantify the impact of your idea on the organization.* This may involve projecting costs, revenues, and return on investment. Or, it may entail estimating non-financial metrics like employee morale, customer satisfaction, product quality, or public relations.

5. *Organize your research and analysis into a formal proposal.* This may take the form of a memo in the case of a proposed change in operating procedures. Or, it may result in a comprehensive business plan when a new product or service is involved.

EXERCISE 6.2

Select an idea that you have been thinking about to enhance your company. Using the methodology discussed in this chapter, take the idea and break it down into smaller tasks. Reward yourself after successfully completing each task. Give yourself a big reward after successfully completing the entire project.

Not all business decisions are proactive and involve proposing new ideas to enhance a business. Many are reactive and are directed toward problem solving. The next case features a manager who lacks self-confidence to solve a chronic employee turnover problem.

Janet is a 34 year-old manager for a large electronics company. She manages the computer-aided design department. During the past two years her department has experienced high employee turnover. Although Janet has made several attempts to rationalize the situation to herself, and her boss, the real issue is her lack of self-confidence in dealing with the problem. Janet has chosen to ignore the problem, in hopes it will go away. Obviously, Janet's behavior in this situation is unacceptable. Now, let's take a look at how Janet should handle the situation. Just like the previous case, once a goal is identified, it must be broken down into smaller parts or manageable tasks.

First, document and understand the problem. What are the actual turnover rates? How do they compare with the other departments in the company? How do they compare with industry averages? What is the cost to the company for high turnover rates?

Second, research the problem. Janet needs to examine the characteristics of the employees who are leaving and look for common denominators such as age, sex, education, job and salary history, pre-employment test scores and interviews, training instructors, type and duration of work assignments, personal time off, disciplinary actions, performance reviews, term of employment, and a host of other variables that may influence job satisfaction. There are many factors that may cause high employee turnover. They include poor employee selection procedures, insufficient training, inadequate supervision, bad working conditions, and limited advancement opportunities. Don't forget exit interviews. Most employees are very honest during an exit interview because they have nothing to lose. Janet may find a common issue such as limited advancement opportunity. Or, she may find that the competition is hiring away many of her best people.

After Janet has examined the employee information, she must take a close look at the competition. She needs to compare wage rates, fringe benefits, and work environment. Sometimes management has blinders on and automatically assumes that everyone wants to work for their company because it is the best in the world. They fail to realize that attractive wage rates, fringe benefits, and work environment are very important in a competitive world.

Third, get others involved in the problem. Janet needs to discuss the situation with her manager and hold some brainstorming sessions with her peers and subordinates. They may suggest additional areas to investigate. Don't consider this a sign of weakness. Managers are not abdicating their responsibility when they ask others for input on problems. They are just practicing good participative management.

Fourth, outline alternative solutions. After Janet has completed a thorough investigation of the problem, and believes she has sufficient insight into the cause of the problem, it's time for her to consider possible solutions. Most problems have more than one possible solution. Janet should outline each solution, along with its advantages and disadvantages, and discuss these solutions with her peers and subordinates. They can help her refine her final recommendation.

It's now time for Janet to take a calculated risk. She may have to present her analysis and recommendation to her manager for final approval. Or, she may have full authority to implement it herself. In either case, she is the one taking the risk. Her recommendation may be rejected, or her decision may be incorrect. However, Janet has taken several important steps to *minimize* this risk. First, she has taken the time to fully understand and document the problem. Second, she has performed a thorough analysis of the problem, looking for the root cause. And third, she has practiced participative management during the investigation of the problem and the formulation of the solution. *Once again, research, planning, and participative management are essential to minimizing risk in business decision-making.*

Let's summarize the steps for *minimizing risk* in problem solving:

1. *Document and understand the problem.* How serious is the problem? What is the financial impact?

2. *Research the problem.* Examine financial data, production schedules, sales trends, or any other information that may help you find the cause of the problem.

3. *Get others involved in the problem.* Discuss it with your boss, and hold brainstorming sessions with your peers and subordinates. Participative manage-

ment will help you refine the analysis of the problem and reduce the risk of your final recommendation.

4. *Outline alternative solutions, each with its advantages and disadvantages.* Discuss these solutions with your peers and subordinates. They can help you improve your final recommendation.

5. *Recommend a solution.* Although you have consulted your manager, peers, and subordinates during the entire problem solving process, the final decision is yours. You are the one responsible for solving the problem and must take full responsibility for the final decision.

EXERCISE 6.3

Select a problem at work that you need to solve (preferably one that you have been avoiding). Using the methodology discussed in this chapter, take the problem and break it down into smaller tasks. Reward yourself after successfully completing each task. Give yourself a big reward after successfully completing the entire project.

You can learn how to take risks and develop your self-confidence in both your personal life and your professional life. Both involve setting realistic goals and then breaking them down into smaller parts or manageable tasks. And, both require the help of others.

People are not born with self-confidence. Others have helped them learn how to take risks throughout their entire lives. Their parents helped them learn how to ride bicycles, play sports, and use power tools. Their teachers helped them build confidence in classroom discussions, group projects, and presentations. Their sports instructors helped them become proficient in sports like tennis, gymnastics, scuba diving, and snow skiing. Their college professors helped them acquire the knowledge and skills necessary to enter the business world. And, their managers, peers, and subordinates helped them succeed in the business world.

Successful executives will tell you that participative management is the key to effective decision-making at all management levels in an organization. In fact, it is even more important at higher levels since the risks are greater. Even corporate presidents minimize the risk of their decisions by consulting with their staff and board of directors. As you can see, the process never ends. From childhood to executive, people will always be there to help you learn how to take risks and become more confident.

CHAPTER HIGHLIGHTS

- Self-confidence is an extension of self-esteem. While self-esteem centers on self-worth, self-confidence deals with the ability to make decisions and take risks.

- Managers with self-confidence are decisive, action-oriented individuals who confront and solve problems instead of worrying about them. In contrast, managers who lack self-confidence are indecisive and doubt their ability to make decisions or solve problems.

- Self-confidence starts in childhood. If your parents gave you the freedom and autonomy to take risks, you began to develop self-confidence at an early age. On the other hand, if your parents were overprotective and sheltered you from new experiences and risks, your self-confidence never had an opportunity to grow.

- Children cannot develop self-confidence without taking risks. However, responsible parents expose their children to controlled risks. They prepare their children for new experiences, and supervise them during these experiences.

- Teachers also play a crucial role in the development of self-confidence. Effective teachers give positive reinforcement to children who take risks and explore new approaches to assignments and problems.

- You cannot develop your self-confidence until you learn how to take risks. There are many types of risks (physical, psychological, financial, etc.). They all involve decision-making and fear of failure.

- Before you can learn how to take risks, you must (1) believe that change is possible, (2) believe that you control your thoughts and feelings, (3) be committed to improving your self-confidence, (4) decide what you want to accomplish and set goals, and (5) have patience.

- You can learn how to take risks and develop self-confidence in both your personal life and your professional life. Both involve setting realistic goals and then breaking them down into manageable tasks.

- There are many activities that you can use to develop personal self-confidence. Sports are a traditional favorite. There are a wide variety of sports activities available, some more risky than others.

- Activities that build personal confidence should possess the following characteristics: (1) risk is moderate, (2) risk is supervised, (3) goal is broken down into smaller tasks, (4) immediate reinforcement for achieving tasks, (5) subsequent tasks involve more risk, and (6) opportunity for continuing development.

- You develop self-confidence in business decisions the same way you develop self-confidence in your personal life. You must learn how to take risks.

- Learning how to take business risks is very similar to learning how to take personal risks. You must determine the areas in which you lack self-confidence and then develop specific goals to address them. Once a goal is identified, it must be broken down into smaller tasks.

- You can minimize your risk of failure in proposing new ideas by (1) limiting the scope of the proposal, (2) researching the feasibility of the idea, and (3) practicing participative management in refining the idea and developing the proposal.

- Not all business decisions are proactive and involve proposing new ideas to enhance a business. Many are reactive and are directed toward problem solving.

- You can minimize your risk of failure in problem solving by (1) documenting and understanding the problem, (2) researching the problem, and (3) practicing participative management in refining the analysis of the problem and outlining alternative solutions.

- People are not born with self-confidence. Others have helped them learn how to take risks and build self-confidence throughout their entire lives. From childhood to executive, people will always be there to help you learn how to take risks and become more confident.

7

ENHANCING YOUR SOCIAL SKILLS

D r. Philip Zimbardo believes there are two major reasons why shy people fail to behave appropriately in social situations. First, their high level of anxiety cripples their ability to talk. And second, they have never mastered the social skills necessary to effectively communicate. Although anxiety-reducing medications and relaxation techniques usually reduce anxiety levels, they do not equip the individual with the social skills they so desperately need. *Shy people avoid social encounters because they have never learned how to meet people, start conversations, and speak up in groups.*

If you have a problem with social skills, you can be helped by simple and effective behavior modification techniques. In order to get more of the social rewards that you want, you must change your behavior patterns in social situations. You will need to learn, practice, and be rewarded for effectively interacting with other people. A successful behavior modification program will also lead to anxiety reduction as self-confidence improves and assertiveness increases.

TREATING THE SYMPTOMS

The vast majority of shy people make some effort to over-come their shyness. Unfortunately, many treat the symptoms of shyness, not the problem. They turn to alcohol, drugs, and forced extroversion for quick solutions. They make themselves go to parties and social functions where they will be surrounded by people. However, they expect that others will approach them and draw them out of their shell. They desperately want to socialize but just don't know how to act. Ultimately, they become frustrated, depressed, and leave the event. Although alcohol and drugs may temporarily remove inhibitions, they don't provide the shy person with the social skills necessary to successfully interact with others.

BREAKING THE ICE

To improve your social skills, you need to start with small goals where your shyness barriers are the least threatening. Striking up short, anonymous conversations with strangers in public places is a good way to begin. At first, quantity is more important than quality. It is practice in "breaking the ice" that you need. Here are some examples:

- When you're checking out at the supermarket look at the cashier's name tag. With a smile on your face, look her directly in the eyes and say, "And how is Sue today?"

- If you have a good experience at a restaurant, ask for the manager when you get ready to leave. Tell him or her about the excellent service and how much you enjoyed the food. It will make the manager feel good as well as yourself.

- When you're paying for your gas at a service station or convenience store, don't just say, "ten dollars on pump six." In addition, comment on the weather. "Have you ever seen so much rain?" "Will it ever stop snowing?" "When will this heat end?"

- The next time you go to an art festival, compliment the artists. Tell them how much you admire their work.

- Go to a home improvement store and ask a clerk for recommendations on a project that you've been thinking about. This might involve updating lighting fixtures, installing a ceiling fan, creating a patio garden, or any other project that you have postponed because you lacked the information necessary to start it.

- If you have a good flight, thank the pilots and flight attendants as you are leaving the plane. Compliment them on the excellent landing and in-flight service.

- When you're waiting in line at the bank, ask the person next to you if he or she knows of a good flower shop in the neighborhood.

- The next time you attend a function involving live entertainment, compliment the performers after the event.

- When you go shopping for new clothes, ask the salesperson for his or her opinion on which colors and styles look good on you.

- The next time you go to a barbershop or hair salon, compliment the barber or stylist.

- When an employee at a fast food restaurant gives you your food, don't just say, "thank you." In addition, say, "have a nice day."

- The next time you go to a car wash, tell the person next to you how much you admire their car.

- When you're waiting in line at a movie theater, ask the person next to you if he or she knows of an ice cream parlor near by.

- When you go to a pharmacy to pick up a prescription, ask the pharmacist some questions about taking the medication. Although this information may already be on the label, most pharmacists will also inform you verbally.

I'm sure you can think of additional situations to practice breaking the ice. The more you practice, the more comfortable you will feel interacting with people. Eventually, it will become a habit, and you will do it naturally.

The main objective of this section is to get you out of your shell and talking to people. All of the examples above involve short, non-threatening situations. The next section will deal with longer conversations where you will learn techniques to keep the conversation flowing.

EXERCISE 7.1

Initiate at least five short, anonymous conversations a day for the next few weeks. You can use the situations in this section or add your own. Make sure you smile and make eye contact. Keep a log of this important social skill activity. Reward yourself for documented progress in breaking the ice. After several weeks this new behavior should become a habit. If not, continue this exercise until it does.

THE ART OF SMALL TALK

Once you've overcome your reluctance to initiate conversations, you can learn how to make *small talk*. You can use small talk in many settings (parties, barber shops and hair salons, health clubs, art and craft shows, business luncheons, conventions and trade shows, etc.). Confident people use small talk every day in their personal life, as well as their professional life, to build common ground with other people. They seem to be able to talk to anyone, and their conversations appear to be fluid and effortless. These successful conversations just don't happen by magic. Confident people use a series of techniques to keep these conversations flowing smoothly.

Dr. Bernardo Carducci believes that one of the most important prerequisites for a successful conversation is a topic of shared interest. After greeting and exchanging names, you need to ask questions and fish around for common ground. "What's your profession, Jim?" "Oh, you're an architect. Where did you go to college?" This may lead to a conversation comparing college experiences. Or, it may lead to a discussion of chosen professions. If these topics don't pan out, you may have to switch to another area like sports, hobbies, homes, children, vacation spots, favorite restaurants, or favorite places to shop. Most people love to talk about their children or favorite vacation spots.

Warning! Avoid your favorite topics, unless they are also your acquaintance's favorite topics. Belaboring a favorite topic does not constitute a conversation. You are talking *at* someone, not *with* them. Although this topic may be a source of security for you, it could be boring for your partner. If it is, you can be sure this will be a short conversation. Also, avoid topics that might be deemed too personal or offensive. In many cases you don't know the background of the other person. If the other person shows signs of surprise or stress (averted eyes, a long pause, blushing, hesitation, or stammering), you may have crossed the line.

Once a topic has been selected, take turns talking and asking questions. Don't dominate the conversation. Also, don't just listen. Look for cues from the other person (such as eye contact or pausing) indicating when they want to talk, and when they want to relinquish the floor to you. When the other person asks you a question, always elaborate on your answer. A simple "yes" or "no" leaves little room to develop a topic.

DEVELOPING SELF-CONFIDENCE IN SMALL TALK

Although the previous section outlines some very effective techniques, you may still be a little nervous about jumping into a conversation. After all, having a conversation with a stranger can be a very frightening event for a shy person. So, the real question is: "How do you develop self-confidence in using these techniques?" The answer should be obvious. The same techniques that you learned in Chapter 6, "Developing Your Self-Confidence," can also be applied to this chapter. Learning social skills is no different than learning SCUBA skills or problem solving skills. You must:

- Establish goals and break them down into smaller, manageable tasks

- Arrange the tasks in ascending order of risk

- Reduce the risks by allowing others
  to help you achieve your goals

- Reward yourself upon successful
  completion of each task

Developing social skills is quite a challenge. You may believe that silence is safer than risking embarrassment or failure. However, you will never become an assertive manager unless you develop your social skills. And, you will never develop your social skills unless you take some risks. Now, let's examine some ways to reduce your anxiety, and minimize your risk of failure, as you learn these important new skills.

First, there are several relaxation exercises that can help you reduce the physical symptoms of anxiety before you engage in a social situation:

- Find a quiet place and comfortable chair. Close
  your eyelids. Take a long, slow deep breath
  through your nose. Breathe out slowly through
  your mouth. Feel the tension leave your body.
  Repeat the exercise until you feel relaxed.

- Imagine yourself in a place where you feel the
  most comfortable. It might be sitting in front of
  a fireplace, or floating on a raft, or taking a stroll
  on a moonlit beach. Whatever your relaxation
  image is, go to it. See it, hear it, smell it, feel it.

- Say self-coping statements like, "I know I can
  do this. I will not feel anxious or tense. I will
  not feel shy. I can get through this." You must
  repeat these statements over and over in your

head. *Remember, you control your thoughts, and your thoughts control your feelings.*

Relaxation exercises are usually very effective in reducing anxiety in social situations. However, if you suffer from high levels of general anxiety, you may require anti-anxiety medication. There's no need to torture yourself when there are prescription medications available to reduce anxiety. These medications will allow you to feel more comfortable during the early phases of your behavior modification program. As you gain confidence in your small talk skills, you can discontinue their use and switch to relaxation exercises. And eventually, as your confidence grows, you may find that even the relaxation exercises are no longer necessary.

Second, pretend you are an actor. Dr. Philip Zimbardo, in his pioneering shyness research, found that role playing was a very effective technique for reducing shyness in social situations. He discovered that role playing allowed many shy people to initiate actions they would never attempt on their own. So, when you start practicing small talk, pretend you are an actor merely playing a role. In acting, or role-playing, you can dissolve the boundary between the so-called *real you* and the *role you play*. In this way, you are not vulnerable, for the real you is not being evaluated.

In role-playing, you must visualize the specific situations and conversations that you would like to engage in, running them through your imagination. Rehearse in front of a mirror, practicing specific lines, gestures, and movements. In the beginning, you will feel more comfortable basing your act on scripts you have prepared in advance. Later on, when your self-confidence increases, you can try more spontaneous, improvised performances. Eventually, you will become comfortable in conversations, and the real you and the role you play will become one and the same.

116

Third, dress for success. Very few of us look like Hollywood movie stars. But each of us can improve on our appearance. Select hairstyles, make-up, and clothes that look good on you. If you aren't sure, ask your friends. Or, better yet, ask a salesperson from one of your favorite stores. This will give you an excellent opportunity to practice small talk. If you want to act assertive, you need to dress for the part.

Fourth, when you start practicing small talk, make sure you begin in comfortable settings. Many traditional parties fall under this guideline: birthdays, graduations, engagements, weddings, showers, and anniversaries. These functions are usually attended by family members and close friends. In the beginning, start your conversations with people you already know. Experiment with some of the techniques that were discussed in the previous section. In order to keep the conversation flowing, remember to ask questions and focus on topics of mutual interest. Talk to lots of people, have fun, and enjoy this learning experience. You will soon discover that success does reinforce success. Each conversation will flow smoother and require less effort on your part.

Continue to practice your new conversation skills as often as you can. When you become comfortable, and confident, talking to people you already know, ask a family member or friend to introduce you to someone new. And, when you feel the time is right, take that big step and introduce yourself to someone new.

After you have experienced a sufficient number of conversations in comfortable settings, it's time to progress to more challenging social situations. These should be places that interest you but aren't as "safe" as your comfortable spots. Here are some places you may want to consider:

- Coffee shops
- Book stores

- Health clubs

- PTA meetings

- Neighborhood association meetings

- Art and craft shows

- Museums

- Sporting events

- Amusement parks

- Civic or social clubs

- Volunteer organizations

These places will give you an opportunity to practice your conversation skills with strangers. Take a friend with you in the beginning. But eventually, you need to go alone in order to develop your self-confidence. Also, I highly recommend joining a social club or volunteer organization. This is an excellent way to meet new people. The phone book will provide you with a listing of all the clubs and organizations in your area. The Internet will give you additional information on many of these organizations.

EXERCISE 7.2

Practice your small talk skills every day. Start out with comfortable places, then progress to those that are less familiar. Keep a record of your conversations. Write down where you went, what happened, and how you felt. Note both positive and negative results. What techniques were successful? What techniques need work? Review your notebook at the end of each week. Reward yourself for documented progress in improving your conversation skills.

SOCIAL SKILLS IN THE WORKPLACE

Work interactions are no different than interactions in your personal life. They follow the same general rules. The social skills you develop in your personal life will easily transfer to your professional life.

Knowing how to communicate with coworkers is essential for gaining the recognition, and help, you need to succeed in your career. A considerable amount of important information is exchanged during breaks, at lunchtime, and after work. Much of this information flows outside official channels. To start conversations with coworkers, follow the same rules for small talk outlined earlier in this chapter. Focus on topics of shared interest. Take turns talking and asking questions. Keep the conversation professional. Match your coworker's level of self-disclosure so you don't get too personal. And, most important, don't engage in gossip. Always keep the conversation positive when discussing your job, coworkers, or the company.

A very important business activity that requires good social skills is *networking*. Networking provides a valuable forum to make business contacts, acquire competitive information, obtain sales leads, and discover job opportunities. Typical events that facilitate networking are:

- Office parties

- Vendor seminars

- Industry conferences

- Trade shows

- Chamber of Commerce events

- Professional association meetings

Networking is a challenge for shy people. It features a room full of strangers, lots of small talk, and many authority figures. Here are some suggestions for navigating this minefield:

- Research the event so you know what to expect.

- Set realistic objectives so you know what you want to accomplish. Start with small goals and build self-confidence.

- Target several people to talk to, and prepare topics and questions.

- Bring a colleague along if it helps you feel more comfortable.

- Practice relaxation exercises before the event.

- Think positive thoughts before and during the meeting. Remember, you control your thoughts.

- Follow the rules of small talk.

- Don't drink! Alcohol interferes with clear thinking. You won't impress anyone if you become sloppy.

- Don't forget the main objective of networking—establishing contacts. Don't worry about solving problems, closing deals, or trying to acquire in-depth information. You can follow up the next day by phone or E-mail.

EXERCISE 7.3

Practice your professional small talk skills every day. Start out with comfortable settings at work, then progress to more threatening situations like networking events. Keep a record of your conversations. Write down where you went, what happened, and how you felt. Note both positive and negative results. What techniques were successful? What techniques need work? Review your notebook at the end of each week. Reward yourself for documented progress in improving your professional conversation skills.

PARTICIPATING IN MEETINGS

Helen is a 28 year-old supervisor who has worked for a life insurance company for the past six years. She has been a supervisor in the information technology department for the past two years. Every two weeks her employees fill out time sheets and submit them to her for approval. After reviewing the entries, she signs each time sheet and forwards them to payroll for processing. A payroll clerk then reviews them and enters the data into the computer payroll system. Helen is convinced that her department could save the company a considerable amount of money if they developed an application that allowed employees to enter their time sheet information directly into their desktop computers. They could then send this information electronically to their supervisor over the computer network. The supervisor could review the data, electronically approve it, and forward it to the payroll department.

This is one of many excellent ideas that Helen has thought of during the past few years. However, Helen is shy and is afraid to bring up her ideas at the weekly staff meetings. Instead, she reports on her projects, and then quietly sits back and listens to other supervisors suggest new systems or recommend improvements on existing ones. Although Helen has been content to operate in this manner in the past, recent events have prompted her to reexamine her participation in staff meetings.

Several weeks ago, Helen discussed her time sheet idea with Robert, another supervisor in the information technology department. Then, to her surprise, Robert presented the concept in the next staff meeting. Their boss loved the idea and assigned Robert to manage the project. Helen sat back quietly while Robert got full credit for the concept. Helen learned a very important lesson the hard way: *You rarely get recognition unless you promote yourself, and you never get the order unless you ask for it.*

Shy people have a difficult time participating in meetings. They often feel their input is unworthy and frequently avoid asking questions because they fear others will consider them stupid. If a superior runs the meeting, that can intensify the fears. In addition, meetings can also be competitive, and stressful, if participants are trying to advance their own agendas. Unfortunately, for the shy participant, silence may be interpreted as disinterest or lack of enthusiasm.

Knowing how to participate in meetings is vital for gaining the recognition you need to succeed in your career. Here are some suggestions for you to review before you attend your next meeting:

- Set several objectives so you know what you want to accomplish. Make sure they are realistic. Start with small goals and build self-confidence.

- Be proactive and contact the chairperson before the meeting. Insert a topic on the agenda that you would like to discuss. Start with minor issues and work your way up to major proposals.

- Prepare for the meeting. Study the agenda, research the topics, and rehearse your questions.

- Practice relaxation exercises before the meeting.

- Think positive thoughts before and during the meeting. *You* control your thoughts.

- Listen carefully during the meeting. As you listen, smile and nod when you agree with a participant.

- Give compliments to participants when appropriate. Make sure they are warranted and sincere. Often, compliments are heard and felt as flattery and as an insincere attempt to manipulate.

- Get involved in the meeting by asking questions. This demonstrates that you're listening to the discussion and gives your colleagues the opportunity to clarify and elaborate on their ideas.

- Act professional and avoid negative comments concerning your job, coworkers, or the company. Ask questions of clarification rather than stating opinions. Never be argumentative or confrontational.

- Promote your ideas so you can receive the recognition that you so rightly deserve. Be receptive to constructive feedback, and never get defensive.

EXERCISE 7.4

Review the suggestions on how to participate in meetings before you attend your next meeting. Continue to review these suggestions before each meeting for the next few months. Repetition is important in changing behavior. Keep a record of your meetings. What suggestions were successful? In what areas do you need to improve? Review your notebook at the end of each week. Reward yourself for documented progress in improving your participation in meetings.

MAKING PRESENTATIONS

Most people fear public speaking—even people who are not shy. The reason is simple. When you make a presentation, *you* are the center of attention, and all eyes are focused on you. A slip of the tongue, or a lapse of memory, may result in embarrassment. People expect you to perform well and say something meaningful. After all, you are the presenter and the expert. This pressure to satisfy the audience, coupled with the fear of embarrassment, creates anxiety in most of us. Although some people savor this spotlight, shy people regard it as torture. They find little pleasure in a pounding heart and a mouth that feels like cotton.

Although making presentations is a challenging task, it is nevertheless a vital prerequisite to becoming a successful manager. Your subordinates need to witness your planning, organization, and leadership skills so they can have confidence in your decisions. Your peers need to be persuaded by the merits of your proposals so they can provide necessary support. And, your superiors need to be impressed by your skill and ability so they can supply required resources.

The single most important objective of a presentation is to make your message *understood* and *remembered*. Therefore, the presentation must be geared to the audience, not the speaker. The presentation of a perfect plan is a failure if the audience is not persuaded to support it. Since the average person has a very short attention span, and many other things to think about, your challenge is to hold their attention long enough to make your point.

Learning how to make effective presentations is no different than learning how to make small talk or participate in meetings. You must establish objectives, learn the necessary skills, minimize unnecessary risks, and reward yourself for achieving your objectives. Gerard Blair, an internationally recognized expert on presentation skills, points out that effective presentations require careful planning and preparation. Before you make your next presentation, you should consider his valuable suggestions:

First, define a *precise* objective. This should take the form of a simple, concise statement. For example, the objective of a presentation may be to explain a new personnel policy, propose a new product, or seek approval for an automation project.

Second, identify the objective of the audience. And, if you can convince them that their objective is the same as yours, you will find a helpful and receptive group. For example, if senior management is currently worried about product quality, you would emphasize this benefit in your automation proposal.

Third, select a structure. A presentation without a structure is like a ship without a rudder. For example, the *problem/solu-*

tion structure introduces a problem and then outlines the advantages and disadvantages of each solution. In the *meaty sandwich* structure, the main meat of the presentation is contained in the middle, preceded by an introduction, and followed by a conclusion.

Fourth, plan a beginning that will get the audience's attention and create a rapport with them. You have only a few minutes to achieve this important objective. This can be easily accomplished by a statement of your objective. And, if their objective is the same as yours, you will have smooth sailing.

Fifth, you must also plan your ending carefully. As Gerard Blair points out, "The final impression you make on the audience is the one they will remember." Your final statements must reinforce your objective. And, these final statements must be delivered with confidence.

Although careful planning and preparation are critical prerequisites for a successful presentation, the proof of the pudding is in the delivery. You are the focus of attention: your eyes, your voice, your expression, and your appearance. Therefore, these facets of the human body deserve special attention:

- Your eyes are your most effective weapon in convincing the audience of your honesty, openness, and confidence in the objective of your presentation. You should establish eye contact with members of the audience as often as possible.

- The two most important aspects of voice in a presentation are *projection* and *variation*. You cannot take your ordinary conversation voice and put it on stage. You should be slightly louder and slightly slower. Also, there is nothing as boring as a monotone speech, so try and vary the pitch and speed of your presentation.

- A facial expression is worth a thousand words. Remember, you are the center of attention, and everyone is watching your face. If you look excited and enthusiastic, then the audience will be excited and enthusiastic. If you look listless and detached, then the audience will be listless and detached.

- The way you dress for a presentation is a matter of personal choice. However, that choice should be deliberately made. You must dress for the audience, not for yourself. If they think you look out of place, then you are. In addition, your posture or stance should convey confidence. Don't pace back and forth waving your hands aimlessly through the air. You must look and act professional at all times.

Effective visual aids can also enhance the delivery of your presentation. Most audiences expect visual reinforcement for any verbal message being delivered. Although a comprehensive discussion of visual aids is beyond the scope of this section, there are a few rules that should be followed to insure that these aids are used effectively:

- Talk to the audience, not the visual aid.

- Use visual aids to reinforce the verbal message, to assist in recall, and to explain information that can be more easily displayed than discussed.

- Keep the text short and concise. Never place more than three or four bullets on a frame.

- Combine graphics and text to keep the presentation interesting.

Learning the above preparation and delivery skills is very important. Developing self-confidence in using these skills is also important. Here are some suggestions for reducing your anxiety, and minimizing your risk of failure, as you learn these important new skills:

- Set realistic objectives. Limit your presentations to small groups in the beginning, where you know most of the people. As you gain confidence, you can progress to larger audiences.

- Pretend you are an actor, playing the role of a presenter. Therefore, you are not vulnerable, for the real you is not in front of the audience being evaluated.

- Practice. Practice. Practice. There is no substitute for rehearsal. To be confident and successful, you must practice your style, pace, tone, and tactics. Practice your gestures in front of a mirror. Then, if possible, test your vocal projection in an empty meeting room.

- Practice relaxation exercises before the presentation.

- Think positive thoughts before and during the presentation. If possible, greet attendees before the presentation. This will give you some familiar faces with whom to make eye contact during the presentation.

- Do not ad-lib or speak off-the-cuff. These are the worst possible speaking strategies for shy people. If you have nothing prepared or rehearsed – you have nothing to say.

- Stop, smile, take a sip of water, breathe deeply, and continue if your voice starts to tremble or your mouth becomes dry. The pause will seem long to you but less so to the audience.

- Take a few minutes and evaluate your performance after each presentation. If you have a friend in the audience, ask him or her to help you. Decide what was the least successful aspect of your presentation and make a personal commitment to improve it.

Without a doubt, making presentations was one of the most difficult obstacles I encountered during my career. When anyone even mentioned the word "presentation," my heart started pounding and my hands started shaking. However, after learning the necessary skills and modifying my self-defeating behavior, I gained self-confidence and started feeling more comfortable in front of groups. Although it was a lot of hard work, and very painful, it was worth it. My ability to make effective presentations gave me a distinct advantage in a very competitive corporate world.

EXERCISE 7.5

The only way to become an effective presenter is to present. Speak as often as you can (at least once a week) at school, social, and company functions. If your speaking opportunities are limited, join a local Toastmasters club, or take a public speaking course from your local community college. Keep a record of your speeches. Ask friends and business colleagues to help you evaluate your performance. Make a personal commitment to improve

in problem areas. Reward yourself for documented progress in improving your presentation skills.

INTERVIEWING

Unfortunately, many talented shy people are stuck in their
job positions because they don't want to undergo the trauma of
job interviewing. Interviews contain the things that shy people
fear the most: lots of small talk, pressure to make a favorable impression, and evaluation by the interviewer. Fortunately, you can
learn how to interview successfully if you are willing to change
your behavior and learn some effective interview skills. The following suggestions are adapted from an excellent article written
by Carole Martin for *MSN Careers*:

- Research the company before the interview. An
  interviewer asking you how you heard about the
  company, or how you think you'll fit in, may
  actually be trying to find out what you know about
  the company. Learning as much as possible about
  the company's mission statement, organization,
  products, services, and culture will give you an edge
  in understanding and addressing the company's
  needs. The more you know about the company, the
  better the chance you have of selling yourself.

- Look sharp, come on time, and be prepared. Select
  a hairstyle, make-up, and clothes that make you
  look professional, confident, and successful. Even
  if the company has a casual environment, wear a
  business suit. You can dress casual once you get

the job. Allow extra time so you can arrive early in the vicinity. Unforeseen problems such as heavy traffic and parking could cause significant delays. Bring extra copies of your resume, a copy of your references, and paper to take notes. Make sure you have questions prepared to ask during the interview. Write them down. Don't rely on your memory.

- Show enthusiasm. Greet the interviewer with a firm handshake and smile. Maintain appropriate eye contact and speak distinctly in a confident voice. An interview is essentially a sales meeting, and the product you are selling is yourself.

- Listen carefully and answer the questions asked. Listening is a neglected interviewing skill. Make sure you know what the interviewer wants to know. Ask for clarification if the question is not clear.

- Give specific examples of your background. One specific example of your background is worth ten vague stories. Interviewers like this behavioral approach because past behavior is usually a good indicator of future performance. So, whenever possible, give specific examples that highlight your successes and uniqueness.

- Ask questions during the interview. Interviewing should be a two-way process. The company is interviewing you, and you should be interviewing the company. Many interviewees don't ask questions and miss the opportunity to find out valuable information about the company. In addition, your questions indicate your interest in the job and the company.

- Ask for the job! Remember the most important principle in sales: "You will never get the order unless you ask for it." During my management career, I was continually amazed that only about ten percent of my interviewees actually asked for the job.

- Follow up after the interview. Whether it's through e-mail or regular mail, the follow-up is one more chance to remind the interviewer of all the valuable traits you bring to the job and the company. Make sure you include in the thank you note some small detail that will help remind the interviewer who you are. A reference to a comment made, or to something that happened during the interview, may help the interviewer connect your name to your face.

Learning effective interview skills is an important prerequisite to advancing your career. Developing self-confidence in using these skills is also important. The following suggestions will help reduce your anxiety and minimize your risk of failure as you learn these important new skills.

First, when it comes to interviews, there is no substitute for preparation. No matter what subject is being discussed, a thoughtful answer should be on the tip of your tongue. Although it is impossible to predict all of the questions in an interview, many common questions can be found in articles on the Internet. Simply search for "Interview Techniques." In addition to listing the questions, many of these articles also offer advice on how to answer them. As you are researching potential questions, select the ones that you want to concentrate on. Write down your answers and rehearse them with a friend. The more you practice, the more confident you will become.

Second, sign up for a mock interview with an interview counseling service. This usually consists of a 30 minute videotaped session where you will be interviewed by a professional interview coach. A week before the mock interview, you will select a job category and company. This will give you time to research the company and prepare answers to possible questions. When the interview is completed, the coach will review the tape with you and provide constructive feedback.

Third, go on practice interviews for positions that only slightly interest you. This will greatly reduce your need for approval and fear of failure. Practice interviews will help acclimate you to the interview process and smooth out rough spots before you attempt an important career move. The more you interview, the easier it will become.

Fourth, make sure you get to the interview location early enough to practice relaxation exercises. They work! Deep breathing exercises can reduce interview anxiety. Taking long, slow deep breaths can have a remarkable calming effect on the body, slowing your heart rate, and decreasing perspiration.

Fifth, think positive thoughts before and during the interview.

EXERCISE 7.6

Practice your interview skills, even if you're satisfied with your current position. You cannot predict when an excellent job opportunity will surface or when you may become dissatisfied with your current position. Review the techniques outlined in this section before each practice interview. Keep a record of your interviews. What techniques were successful? In what areas doyou need to improve? Reward yourself for documented progress in improving your interview skills.

PRACTICE MAKES PERFECT

You will never become an effective manager unless you develop your social skills. And, you will never develop your social skills unless you practice the exercises in this chapter. Simply reading the exercises will not suffice. You must do them. Also, focus on one exercise at a time. Remember, to be successful, you must break your goals down into smaller, manageable tasks. The successful completion of one exercise will motivate you to start the next one. Success will reinforce success. Change is not easy, and it does not come fast. If you have realistic expectations, and are dedicated to improving your social skills, I am confident that you will succeed.

CHAPTER HIGHLIGHTS

- There are two major reasons why shy people fail to behave appropriately in social situations. First, their high level of anxiety cripples their ability to talk. And second, they have never mastered the social skills necessary to effectively communicate.

- Many shy people treat the symptoms of shyness, not the problem. They turn to alcohol, drugs, and forced extroversion for quick solutions. Unfortunately, these solutions don't provide the shy person with the social skills necessary to successfully interact with others.

- To improve your social skills, you need to start with small goals where your shyness barriers are the least threatening. Striking up short, anonymous conversations with strangers in public places is a good way to begin.

134

- Once you've overcome your reluctance to initiate conversations, you can learn how to make small talk. In making small talk, you must (1) look for topics of shared interest, (2) avoid your favorite topics, (3) avoid controversial topics, and (4) take turns talking and asking questions,

- You can reduce your anxiety and fear of failure as you learn small talk by (1) practicing relaxation exercises, (2) utilizing role-playing, (3) improving your appearance, and (4) beginning your small talk exercises in comfortable settings.

- The social skills you develop in your personal life will easily transfer to your professional life. To start conversations with coworkers, follow the same rules used for personal small talk.

- Other business activities that require good social skills are networking, participating in meetings, making presentations, and interviewing.

- To improve your networking skills, you must (1) research the event, (2) set realistic objectives, (3) target several people to talk to, and (4) focus on establishing contacts. Don't try to solve problems or close deals.

- To improve your participation in meetings, you must (1) set realistic objectives, (2) be proactive concerning the agenda, (3) prepare for the meeting, (4) listen carefully during the meeting, (5) give compliments to participants when appropriate, (6) get involved and ask questions, (7) act professional and avoid negative comments, and (8) promote your ideas.

- To improve your presentation skills, you must (1) define a precise objective, (2) identify the objective of the audience, (3) select an appropriate presentation structure, (4) plan a beginning that will get the audience's attention, and (5) plan an ending that will make a lasting impression.

- Successful presentations also require effective delivery. You must (1) establish eye contact as often as possible, (2) project your voice and vary the pitch and speed, (3) look excited and enthusiastic, and (4) dress for the audience, not for yourself.

- You can reduce your anxiety and fear of failure as you learn presentation skills by (1) setting realistic objectives, like starting with small groups, (2) practicing relaxation exercises, (3) utilizing role-playing, (4) practicing your delivery, (5) greeting attendees before the presentation, (6) refraining from ad-libbing or speaking off-the-cuff, and (7) taking a sip of water, or breathing deeply, if your voice starts to tremble or your mouth becomes dry.

- To improve your interviewing skills, you must (1) research the company, (2) look sharp, come on time, and be prepared, (3) show enthusiasm, (4) listen carefully and answer the questions asked, (5) give specific examples of your background, (6) ask questions during the interview, (7) ask for the job, and (8) follow up after the interview.

- You can reduce your anxiety and fear of failure as you learn interviewing skills by (1) practicing relaxation exercises, (2) thinking positive thoughts before and during the interview, (3) researching potential questions, (4) signing up for a mock interview, and (5) going on practice interviews.

PART III

MANAGING ASSERTIVELY

8

ASKING FOR WHAT YOU WANT

There have been numerous books and articles written on assertiveness. They offer suggestions and techniques on how to become a more assertive child, parent, spouse, relative, neighbor, consumer, citizen, worker, and so on. The list is endless. All of these publications have one thing in common—they advocate standing up for yourself and making your views heard and understood. Although many of these assertive topics will help you in your personal life, they are beyond the scope of this book. The objective of Part III, "Managing Assertively," is to help you in your professional life. This section will focus on three of the most important topics in the assertive management area:

- Asking For What You Want

- Learning How to Say No

- Correcting Employee Behavior

It's now time for you to take the next step in your development program and start acting more assertively. That's right—I said *acting*. In the last chapter you discovered that acting, or role-playing, can help you dissolve the boundary between the so-called *real you* and the *role you play.* You can also use role-playing in this chapter to help you learn assertiveness techniques. Role-playing will allow you to minimize your risk in learning these techniques by making you less vulnerable, for the real you is not being judged or evaluated. Eventually, you will become more comfortable using these techniques, and the real you and the assertive role that you play will become one and the same.

Assertiveness has a major influence on how fast, and how high, you climb the corporate ladder. Numerous studies have shown that if two managers have similar education, experience, and accomplishments, the one who is more assertive will rise faster in his or her career. Why are assertive managers so successful? The answer is simple. They are not afraid to *ask for what they want.* They do not hesitate to ask their superiors for necessary resources. Nor, are they reluctant to ask their peers for help and support on important proposals and projects. And, they are not afraid to ask their subordinates to do whatever it takes to get the job done. In short, assertive managers are very successful at influencing others. Their confident and honest approach toward interpersonal relationships wins them respect at all levels in the organization.

THE ART OF DELEGATION

Management is often defined as "getting things done through people." However, many shy managers and supervisors feel uncomfortable asking for what they want. They are often haunted by childhood messages that remind them that it's not OK to ask for what they want. Fortunately, the self-defeating habits acquired in childhood can be replaced with more constructive ones later in life. Asking for what you want is no exception. You can unlearn old behaviors and replace them with new ones that will help you become a more effective manager. In order to accomplish this, you must learn assertive skills and be rewarded for practicing them in management situations. Here are seven important guidelines for asking *assertively* for what you want:

- Never delegate your responsibility for assigning tasks. Delegating is your job.

- Assign the right person to each task.

- Use physical and vocal assertiveness to project authority.

- Ask specifically for *what* you want, *when* you want it, and *why* you want it.

- Don't be afraid to assign unpleasant tasks.

- Never let a subordinate delegate back to you.

- Monitor the progress on all assigned tasks.

Each of these guidelines will be examined in more detail in the following sections. Each section will contain a case study, as well as suggestions to help you learn these important skills.

DELEGATING IS YOUR JOB

Eric was promoted two years ago to supervise a group of eight computer support technicians in a government agency. When computer users in the agency experience a hardware or software problem, they call the support group help desk. The technician on duty records all of the pertinent information from the caller and creates a service ticket. During his first year as supervisor, Eric personally assigned each service ticket to a technician for resolution. However, during the past year, Eric has delegated the assignment of problem calls to Greg, one of his senior technicians.

Eric discovered early in his supervisory role that managing people is not easy. And, managing people when you are shy is downright painful. Members of his group were always complaining about assignments. Some felt that many of the assignments were too difficult based on their experience and skill level. Others believed that many of their assignments were boring and not challenging. Eric would often reassign problem calls based on which technician complained the loudest. In addition, Eric would sometimes forget that he already assigned a technician to a call and would assign another technician to the same call. This was particularly frustrating when the call came from a remote location. Also, Eric would frequently fail to communicate the urgency and priority of a problem call. Since most technicians were assigned multiple calls during any given day, this often created unnecessary confusion. After a year of frustration and stress, Eric decided to delegate the assignment of problem calls to Greg.

Greg had no problem handling the assignment. He was very assertive and possessed excellent people skills. He quickly discovered that many of the technicians' complaints stemmed from a lack of communication between Eric and the group. After several months, the assignment problem had practically disappeared, and the morale of the group was greatly improved. Although Eric indirectly solved the assignment problem by delegating the task to Greg, he soon discovered that he created a more serious problem. Members of the group became comfortable taking work direction from Greg and started interfacing directly with him on other group activities and issues.

How prevalent is this situation in organizations? More than you would expect. I have witnessed many shy managers like Eric abdicate one or more of their major management responsibilities to a subordinate. It doesn't take long for the subordinate to become the informal leader of the group relegating the formal manager impotent and ineffective.

The lesson to be learned from the above case is very simple. *Never* delegate your responsibility for assigning tasks. If you do, your employees will soon lose respect for you and quickly turn to someone else in the group for leadership. If you have a problem delegating work assignments to your employees, treat the problem, not the symptoms. Learn the necessary skills for effective delegation.

ASSIGNING THE RIGHT PERSON

Steve manages a product development group in a consumer electronics company. The group typically has eight to ten projects in the development cycle. Approximately half the projects are new products, while the other half are enhancements to existing products. Steve always assigns the new products to senior engineers who have been with the company for five years or longer. He justifies this approach by pointing out that new products are more difficult to design and require engineers who are more experienced with the company culture. In reality, Steve is intimidated by the senior engineers and usually makes project assignments based on their recommendations.

Alex joined the group three years ago. He is an outstanding engineer with ten years of experience in designing consumer electronics. He just finished his third product enhancement project. All three were extremely successful. Alex has become increasingly frustrated with Steve's assignment policy and has started looking for another job. He is not alone. Two other bright young engineers have left the group during the past six months.

Consistently assigning the right person to a task is not easy. You must balance employee qualifications with the need to gain experience in new situations. Although your senior employees may be more qualified to head up a new project, you must give your employees with less experience an opportunity to improve their skills and show what they're really capable of doing. Mary Albright and Clay Carr, authors of *101 Biggest Mistakes Managers Make*, offer some valuable suggestions to help you consistently and assertively select the right person for each task:

First, review the qualifications of each of your employees. Examine their education and experience, and list their specific skills. Also, identify their potential by listing other skills they *could* develop if given the proper education and training.

Second, review the assignments of everyone in your group. Have you been fair? Do you see imbalances? Do you give the "interesting" and "challenging" assignments to the same few people over and over again?

Third, develop an effective *task distribution* process. If most of the employees in your group have similar qualifications, set up a rotating list for new assignments. Don't cheat! If a special assignment comes in, and it's Mark's turn, don't give it to Sue simply because you have a "gut feeling" that she would do a better job. Mark must have the opportunity to grow and be held accountable for his performance. If the work in your group is specialized, you should identify opportunities for cross training.

PROJECTING PHYSICAL ASSERTIVENESS

Ken supervises a group of ride operators at a theme park. Although Ken is six-foot-two and weighs 200 pounds, he is not physically or vocally assertive. He walks with his shoulders slumped forward and constantly looks down. When he talks to his employees he avoids eye contact and frequently stumbles over his words. He uses sentences punctuated by "um," "err," and "ah." Ken's employees do not take him seriously. They interrupt him during meetings and make fun of him behind his back. And, he has to ask them several times before they will perform a task.

Physical size does not equate to physical assertiveness. Ken's body language and speech send a clear message to his employees that he is insecure and lacks self-confidence. The key to projecting greater physical and vocal assertiveness is self-awareness. Following is a checklist to help you with your self-assessment:

- Keep your head up, shoulders back, and walk with an even stride.

- Take the initiative to heartily greet others and firmly shake hands.

- Make eye contact, speak with authority, and use clear, resonant tones. Eliminate sentences punctuated by "um," "err," and "ah."

- Use moderate hand and arm gestures to make a point. Don't wave your hands aimlessly through the air.

- Maintain good posture. Sit up straight in your chair, and don't lean on the wall, or a table, when standing and conversing with others.

ASKING SPECIFICALLY FOR WHAT YOU WANT

Chris is a district manager for a life insurance company. In preparation for an important staff meeting with his boss, he asked his administrative assistant to prepare a report for him. The conversation went like this:

CHRIS: (looking at the wall)
"Betty, if it's not too much trouble, could you please get me current sales figures for all of the offices in our district."

BETTY: "When do you need them?"

CHRIS: "I have a meeting with Mr. Williams on Friday at 11:00 a.m., so I'll need the numbers by 9:00 a.m. so I can review them."

CHRIS: (Friday at 9:15 a.m.)
"Betty, these sales numbers are from last month. I need fiscal year-to-date numbers so they can be compared to last year. Can you get me the right numbers by 11:00?"

BETTY: "I'm sorry, Chris. When you asked for current sales figures, I thought you meant last month. I don't think we can get year-to-date numbers from accounting by 11:00."

What did Chris do wrong? Although he told Betty when he needed the information, and why he needed it, he did not specify *clearly* what he needed. He should have specifically asked for fiscal year-to-date numbers. Also, Chris did not assertively ask for what he needed. While he was looking at the wall, he apologetically asked Betty for the information. Here are some suggestions to help you assertively ask for what you want and hopefully avoid confusing situations like the one above:

- Project physical and vocal assertiveness when asking for what you want. Your nonverbal behavior should match your words.

- Ask specifically for what you want, when you want it, and why you want it. Employees can't read your mind.

- Never assign a task to an employee and tell him or her that *your* boss wants it done. Delegation is your responsibility. Don't pass the buck.

- If appropriate, ask your employee at the end of the request what they expect to give you and when.

- If necessary, and the situation warrants it, write your request down.

ASSIGNING UNPLEASANT TASKS

Martha supervises a group of deli clerks in a supermarket. Every night after closing, the equipment needs to be cleaned, especially the slicing machines. Martha always helps with cleanup and assigns herself the most unpleasant task—cleaning the slicing machines. Each machine must be taken apart, cleaned, and then reassembled. Martha believes it's important for a supervisor to "lead by example." She wants to show the group that just because she's the boss, she is not "too good" to roll up her sleeves and help during cleanup.

Martha has convinced herself that she needs to clean the slicing machines to facilitate group camaraderie. In reality, Martha cleans the slicing machines because she is afraid to assign this task to someone else. She has a strong need for approval, and wants everyone in the group to like her. Unfortunately, Martha has achieved her objective. Everyone in the group does like her; however, *they don't respect her.*

Martha has a very distorted understanding of "leading by example." Employees look to a supervisor for leadership. They want a supervisor to be honest, trustworthy, and fair. When a supervisor acts like an employee and wants to be "one of the group," the group soon loses respect for the supervisor.

The above case demonstrates a specific situation where a shy supervisor is afraid to delegate a cleaning task. Shy supervisors also feel uncomfortable delegating other types of unpleasant assignments. They include:

- Routine, boring tasks

- Undesirable shifts (late night, weekends, holidays, etc.)

- Mandatory overtime

- Business travel

- Additional tasks due to temporary employee shortages (sick leave, vacations, terminations, etc.)

- Increased responsibilities as a result of downsizing (top management asks the organization to do more with less)

Assigning unpleasant tasks is a management responsibility. In order to become a more effective manager in this area, you must unlearn old behaviors and replace them with new ones. Here is a checklist to help you assertively assign unpleasant tasks:

- Use physical and vocal assertiveness to project authority.

- Be fair and rotate the unpleasant assignments.

- Ask specifically for what you want, when you want it, and why you want it.

- Plan your employees' work schedules and assignments carefully. Give them advanced notice on things like schedule changes, additional workload, and travel.

- Thank your employees after they complete an unpleasant task. Tell them how much you appreciate their professionalism and commitment to the organization.

AVOIDING REVERSE DELEGATION

Randy is the manager of human resources for a metropolitan police department. During the past six months he has noticed that it's become increasing difficult to recruit police officers. To help solve this problem, he recently asked his administrative assistant to research current pay ranges at other police departments in the state. The conversation went like this:

RANDY: "Linda, during the past six months I've noticed that it's become increasing difficult to recruit police officers. Perhaps our pay ranges are out of line with other agencies in the state. Would you please contact these ten police departments and find out their current pay ranges. Also, ask them how they adjust the starting pay based on years of experience. I need this information in two weeks. Thanks."

LINDA: "Randy, are you sure you want me to do this? Maybe they would rather be contacted by you than someone at my level."

RANDY: "Maybe you're right. I'll give you the data when I'm finished so you can summarize the results."

Well, who's the boss, and who's the employee? Although Randy did a good job of asking Linda specifically for what he wanted, when he wanted it, and why he wanted it, Linda sure turned the tables on him. When you allow an employee to delegate back to you, you become the employee, and the employee becomes the boss. So, how do you avoid reverse delegation? Here are some suggestions to help you deal with this situation.

First, politely, but firmly, refuse the reverse delegation. Once you accept reverse delegation, you set a dangerous precedent, and it will grow. In the above case, Randy could have responded, "Yes, Linda, I'm sure that I want you to contact them. I'm confident that you have the ability to complete this project."

Second, overcome the employee's objection. When Linda stated, "Maybe they would rather be contacted by you than someone at my level," Randy could have responded, "When you call each police department, make sure you tell them that you're my administrative assistant. When you use my name and title, I'm sure you'll get the cooperation you need."

Third, whenever possible, assign your employees complete projects. Employees, who are assigned whole projects, or a substantial segment, are less likely to try reverse delegation. No one wants to handle uninteresting details or grunt work.

MONITORING PROGRESS

Susan supervises a group of eight computer programmers in a corporate information technology department. Two months ago, she assigned Joan a project to revise the payroll system. Susan described each change very carefully and gave Joan an opportunity to ask questions. She also emphasized the importance of the project and stated that it must be completed in three months. Susan recently called Joan into her office to review the project and discovered that it was only half finished. Susan became extremely frustrated and lashed out at Joan, "If you were having problems, why didn't you come to me?"

Where did Susan go wrong? Although she communicated to Joan what she wanted, when she wanted it, and why she wanted it, she failed to devise a plan to monitor her progress. Here are some guidelines to keep you from making this mistake.

First, keep close enough tabs on the project so you'll recognize if it's having problems. However, don't micromanage or constantly look over your employee's shoulder. If you monitor a project too closely, you may annoy your employee and negatively impact his or her productivity.

Second, schedule a series of review meetings when you initially assign the project. Schedule the meetings at regular intervals, and make sure the intervals are short enough to allow for problem recognition and resolution.

Third, don't hesitate to call unscheduled meetings if the situation warrants it. Some projects are fluid, and the requirements may change in mid-stream.

EXERCISE 8.1

Make a list of the seven guidelines for asking assertively for what you want. Place this list in the top middle drawer of your desk. Review this list before you delegate a task. Keep a logbook on all delegated tasks. After each task is successfully completed, give yourself a grade on each of the seven guidelines. Reward yourself for documented progress in asking assertively for what you want.

ASKING YOUR PEERS

Asking for what you want is not limited to your subordinates. You must also learn how to assertively ask your peers for what you want. Your success as a manager depends on your ability to effectively interact with other managers. Many tasks and projects require the assistance of other departments. If you cannot influence these managers to give you the necessary support, your project is doomed from the start. For example, the human resources department usually recruits and screens applicants for all departments in an organization. If they give you a low priority, you will not be able to fill your positions and meet your objectives. The information technology department also plays a key role in most organizations. They must provide you with the computer resources required to bring your projects in on time and within budget. And, let's not forget the finance department.

They process your purchase orders, expense reports, and many other critical financial transactions. To be successful, you must effectively interact with all of the above departments, as well as a host of other departments in your organization.

In addition to asking managers in other departments for the resources you need, you should also consult with these peers on important decisions. In Chapter 6, "Developing Your Self-Confidence," you learned that participative management is essential to minimizing risk in decision-making. Whether it's refining an idea for a new product or fine tuning the analysis of a problem, asking your peers for input will ultimately lead to better decisions.

How do you assertively ask your peers for what you want? In many cases, the same way you ask your subordinates. There is, however, one important difference. Your subordinates report directly to you—your peers do not. It's much easier for a peer to say no than a subordinate. Therefore, your real challenge is to assertively influence your peers to do what you want. You can accomplish this objective by using several of the guidelines discussed in the previous section.

First, never ask one of your subordinates to make a request to one of your peers. That is your job. If you delegate this task to a subordinate, your peer may perceive this request to be less important and give it a low priority. Also, both your peer and your subordinate may lose respect for you since you are abdicating your management responsibility. And, most important of all, how are you ever going to build close working relationships with your peers if you don't communicate directly with them?

Second, use physical and vocal assertiveness to project authority. Speak with authority, and project confidence with your body language. The physical and vocal techniques discussed in the previous section apply to peers as well as subordinates. You will not gain the respect and cooperation of your peers if you don't speak and act assertive.

Third, ask specifically for what you want, when you want it, and why you want it. Simple requests can be handled verbally, but complex requests should always be conveyed in writing. Also, your peers will give your request a higher priority if you can point out something in the request that will benefit them or their department. And last, don't forget that cooperation is a two-way street. If you respond to their requests in an accurate and timely fashion, they will do likewise.

Fourth, monitor the progress of your requests. Although the due date should be mutually agreeable, build in some slack time just in case the peer runs into an unexpected situation. Periodically check with the peer to obtain an informal status of the request. However, don't monitor the request too closely. You may irritate him or her and strain your working relationship.

ASKING YOUR BOSS

Asking your boss for what you want is a critical management function. While some of these requests may be routine in nature, others are very complex and may involve major capital expenditures. Here are some examples of what managers typically ask for:

- Additional personnel to support company growth

- Increased capital for new equipment, automation projects, and expansion programs

- Guidance in resolving major personnel issues

- Assistance in solving project problems

- Support for internal transfers and promotions

- Approval for attending training seminars, industry conferences, and trade shows

- Increased salary, bonuses, and stock options

- Time off for vacations and other events

Asking your boss for what you want can be an anxiety-laden event. After all, he or she has authority over you that other people don't have. For example, your manager has the power to fire you. In addition, your manager conducts performance appraisals of you that impact your compensation and ability to advance in the organization. Although these factors tend to inhibit assertive behavior, you cannot let them deter you from asserting yourself with your manager.

The key to becoming more assertive with your manager is *communications*. You must lay the foundation of *accountability* and *trust* before you seek to assert yourself. Here are some important tips:

- Learn your manager's communication style. Thus, if your manager prefers to "warm up" and chat for a few minutes, don't rush your agenda. However, if he or she prefers to get "right to business," then proceed full speed ahead.

- Acknowledge all requests from your manager in a timely manner. Give them your highest priority. If your manager has given you multiple assignments, make sure you understand the priority of each. If there is any doubt, ask your manager to clarify the priorities.

- Keep your manager informed on the status of all assignments. If there is any significant change, either positive or negative, promptly notify your manager.

- Complete all of your assignments on time. This is an important prerequisite for developing credibility and trust with your manager.

- Keep your manager informed on all significant activities in your organization. Never let your manager hear about a problem from someone else. Managers don't like surprises.

- Take personal responsibility for all activities (good or bad) in your organization. Nothing lays the groundwork better for you to be assertive with your boss than taking full responsibility for your actions.

- Be open and honest with problems. Never hide problems from your manager. They will ultimately surface and erode your credibility.

- Be open and honest with permissions. It is *not* "easier to get forgiveness than it is to get permission." This is usually a *fatal* mistake.

- Dress and act professional at all times. Apply the physical and vocal assertiveness techniques discussed earlier in this chapter.

- Listen carefully when your manager is conversing with you. Don't interrupt, and never argue. (The sensitive topic of "disagreeing with your boss" will be covered in the next chapter).

- Compliment your manager when he or she warrants it. Your boss is a person, too, and needs positive strokes just like everyone else.

EXERCISE 8.2

Make a list of the above guidelines for improving your accountability and trust. At the end of each week, give yourself a grade on each guideline. Place each sheet in a notebook so you can track these self-evaluations. Reward yourself for documented progress in improving your communication with your boss.

MINIMIZING YOUR RISK

Once you have laid the groundwork for improving your communication, you can start to build self-confidence in asserting yourself with your boss. However, as you'll recall from previous chapters, you can't build self-confidence unless you are willing to take some risks. So, let's examine some ways to reduce your anxiety, and minimize your risk of failure, in asking your boss for what you want.

First, develop a plan to become more assertive with your boss. Set objectives so you know what you want to accomplish. Start with small goals and build self-confidence. Remember, success reinforces success.

Second, prepare for the meetings. If you're asking for approval on a decision, come to the meeting armed with supporting documentation. Map out the costs and benefits as accurately and succinctly as you can. Rehearse the meeting ahead of time, practicing specific lines, gestures, and movements. Anticipate your boss's objections and practice your responses.

Third, practice relaxation exercises before the meetings. In addition, think positive thoughts before and during the meetings. Remember, you control your thoughts, and your thoughts control your feelings. If you think and act self-confident, you will project that image to your boss. And, in most cases, you will get what you want.

Fourth, ask assertively for what you want. Don't sell yourself short. You may have more leverage with your boss than you think. In fact, your boss may be more dependent on you than you are on him or her.

To be effective in your position, you must be assertive with your boss. If you are not, you will ultimately fail in many of your objectives. The following cases vividly demonstrate this point.

ASKING FOR ASSISTANCE

Howard is a district sales manager for a computer manufacturing company. He supervises eight sales representatives. During the past six months, one of Howard's sales representatives, Tom, has been working with a distributor of automotive parts. The distributor is looking to replace their current computer system with a more powerful mainframe. The value of this sales opportunity is approximately two million dollars. Both Howard and Tom have spent a considerable amount of time on this opportunity. They have analyzed the system requirements and have proposed an excellent solution for a very attractive price. In addition, they have established an excellent rapport with the distributor's director of information technology. Howard is convinced that his company will win the order.

Unfortunately, Howard was wrong. The distributor chose a

competitor for the new computer system. How did Howard lose such a sure opportunity? He violated one of the cardinal rules of sales—"Never lose one by yourself." You can win as many as you want by yourself, but never lose one by yourself. While Howard was focusing on the director of information technology, Richard, the district sales manager of the winning company, was busy asking his superiors for assistance. He arranged for the regional sales manager, the vice president of sales, and the president, to visit the distributor. They all met with the distributor's top management team and discussed the importance of support, trust, and long-term working relationships.

Although Howard had a better technical solution, at a very attractive price, he did not take advantage of his top management team to close this important opportunity. Never hesitate to involve upper management in major sales opportunities. They will do whatever is necessary for you, and the company, to be successful. And, they also enjoy the recognition and spotlight.

ASKING FOR ADDITIONAL RESOURCES

Mary is a project manager for a large construction company. The company specializes in road and bridge construction. Mary has been managing a large bridge renovation project for the past six months. John, the division manager, recently discovered that the project was a month behind schedule. He called Mary into his office. The conversation went like this:

JOHN: "Mary, I just received the monthly project status reports and discovered that your project is a month behind schedule. What's the problem?"

MARY: (looking at the papers on John's desk) "I'm sorry, John. We just can't seem to finish the structural analysis phase. Maybe if the project had another structural engineer we could complete this phase."

JOHN: "Why didn't you come to me and ask for additional resources?"

MARY: "I was afraid of cost overruns, and, besides, I thought we could make up the time."

JOHN: "Mary, you know that this is a cost-plus contract. You should have asked for another engineer. Now we have a major problem."

How did Mary wind up in this predicament? First, she underestimated the resources required to complete this project on time. Second, when she realized that she needed another engineer, she failed to go to her manager and make the request. And third, she failed to keep her manager informed on the status of the project. Remember, never let your manager hear about a problem from someone else. Managers don't like surprises.

ASKING FOR A RAISE

George is a store manager for a national fast-food chain. He has been in this position for two years. His annual review at the end of his first year reflected average performance, and he received a four percent merit increase. George was satisfied with this increase because he was still learning the operation and felt there was room for improvement. Although his sales and profit results were acceptable, they were near the low end of the company target range.

George's store showed excellent improvement during his second year. Both sales and profit exceeded the company target range. All aspects of his operation were running smooth, and he was confident that his annual merit increase would be eight to ten percent. Unfortunately, when he received his annual review, he discovered that his increase was only five percent—significantly lower than he had expected.

Why didn't George get the raise he expected? The answer is simple. He did not ask for it. Don't assume that outstanding job performance will automatically get you an excellent raise. No matter how hard you work, and how much the company benefits from you, it takes more than wishful thinking to get you a good raise. Here are some suggestions to help you get the compensation that you deserve:

- Be proactive and seek out your boss several months before the review. Don't wait until the annual review. Once the annual review occurs, it's often too late to make changes in the company compensation plan.

- Apply the physical and vocal assertiveness techniques discussed earlier in this chapter. Be assertive and ask for what you want.

- Discuss your accomplishments and demonstrate your value. Have the facts to back it up. Bring a list of accomplishments, projects done on time, and any other data that shows your contribution to the bottom line.

- Determine your market value by checking online job sites and salary surveys. However, be careful how you use this information. Some managers may perceive this as "blackmail" or an indirect threat to leave.

- Don't vent your frustrations by threatening to leave.

Although you may succeed in the short-run, you will damage your long-term relationship with your boss.

- Practice the important suggestions discussed earlier in this chapter. Asking for a raise can be less intimidating if you have a good relationship with your boss. To accomplish this, you must lay the foundation of accountability and trust.

- Turn a refusal into a positive situation. If your boss tells you that you don't deserve more money, ask how you can improve the situation. Or, if your boss says the timing is bad, ask when the timing will be better.

EXERCISE 8.3

Review this section before you ask your boss for what you want, especially the tips on minimizing your risk of failure. Keep a journal on your requests. Record the request and the outcome. What techniques were successful? In what areas do you need to improve? Reward yourself for documented progress in asking your boss for what you want.

CHAPTER HIGHLIGHTS

- Assertive managers are more successful because they are not afraid to "ask for what they want." If two managers have similar education, experience, and accomplishments, the one who is more assertive will rise faster in his or her career.

- Assertive managers never delegate their responsibility for assigning tasks. If they do, their employees will soon lose respect for them and quickly turn to someone else in the group for leadership.

- Assertive managers select the right employee for each assignment. They examine past employee assignments, review current employee qualifications, and maintain an effective task distribution process.

- Assertive managers project physical and vocal assertiveness. They keep their heads up, shoulders back, and walk with an even stride. They also make eye contact, speak with authority, and use clear, resonant tones.

- Assertive managers ask specifically for what they want, when they want it, and why they want it. Failure to clearly communicate requests usually results in incomplete or unacceptable work.

- Assertive managers are not afraid to assign unpleasant tasks. They recognize that most employees don't have a problem with these tasks as long as the assignments are made equitably.

- Assertive managers never let an employee delegate back to them. They always find a way to politely, but firmly, refuse the reverse delegation and overcome the employee objection.

- Assertive managers monitor the progress on all assigned tasks. They use scheduled and unscheduled meetings to identify potential problems.

- Asking for what you want is not limited to your

subordinates. You must also learn how to assertively ask your peers, and your boss, for what you want.

- Your success as a manager depends on your ability to effectively interact with other managers. Many tasks and projects require the assistance of other departments. If you cannot influence these managers to give you the necessary support, your project is doomed from the start.

- Your peers will give your request a higher priority if you can point out something in the request that will benefit them or their department. Also, don't forget that cooperation is a two-way street. If you respond to their requests in an accurate and timely fashion, they will do likewise.

- The key to becoming more assertive with your manager is communications. You must lay the foundation of accountability and trust before you seek to assert yourself.

- You can develop a trusting relationship with your boss if you (1) learn your manager's communication style, (2) promptly acknowledge all requests from your manager, (3) keep your manager informed on the status of all significant assignments and activities in your group, (4) complete all of your assignments on time, (5) take personal responsibility for all activities in your group, and (6) always be open and honest with your manager.

9

LEARNING HOW TO SAY NO

"**N**o, I just don't have time to help you today. How about tomorrow afternoon?" Assertive managers use simple phrases like this every day to deny requests. Shy managers, on the other hand, have a difficult time using the word "no." They allow themselves to be manipulated by guilt, anger, and tears. Their strong need for approval, and fear of rejection, stop them from saying "no." And, when they do say "no," they are riddled with guilt.

Each time you give into your fear of rejection and say "yes," the short-term anxiety reduction merely reinforces your "yes-saying" habit. But, the longer-term consequences of your self-defeating behavior are costly. If you say "yes," especially when you want to say "no," you will eventually discover that you are no longer in charge of your own life.

It's time for you to stop this self-defeating behavior, to stop the need for approval and the fear of rejection. To become an assertive manager, you must learn how to say "no" to your subordinates, your peers, and your superiors.

GUIDELINES FOR SAYING NO

There are many formats for saying "no." You must carefully choose the one that best suits the person and the situation. Here are some guidelines to help you learn how to say "no."

- Give yourself time to review the request. This may simply be a few seconds to interrupt your reflex "yes" response, or it may be a few days so you can carefully analyze all aspects of the request. Also, if you do delay the response, make sure you tell the person when you are going to respond.

- Plan your response. Decide *what* you want to say and *how* you want to say it. If you stammer or hesitate during your response, you will project uncertainty and may open the door for a challenge.

- Use assertive body language. Make direct eye contact, keep your head up, shoulders back, and hands relaxed or gesturing normally. Speak with authority and use clear, resonant tones. If you say "no" with your words and "maybe" with your body, the person will believe your body and challenge your response.

- Try to find an alternative if you cannot agree to a request. For example: "No, I just don't have time to attend the project review next Wednesday. Can I send my assistant?"

- Briefly clarify your reasons if you respond with a "no" and can't offer an alternative. Do not include lengthy excuses, justifications, or rationalizations. And, never say "I'm sorry." Apologetic phrases merely weaken your stand. Your response should be polite but firm. For example: "Ann, I can't ap-

prove your request to attend the NETCOM conference in Chicago. We are currently over budget and
must reduce training and conference expenses."

- Shift the burden of the request back to the person
if the situation warrants it. For example: "Ted, I
just received your purchase requisition for a laptop
computer. These computers are twice as expensive
as the desktops. If I approve this requisition, everyone in the office will want a laptop computer.
Do you think this is fair to the other employees?"

- Use the *broken record response* when dealing with
very aggressive or manipulative people who "won't
take no for an answer." Select a brief statement and
calmly repeat it after each request. For example:

RON: "I'm not interested in the product."

MIKE: "Would you like me to leave a demo for
a week?"

RON: "I'm not interested in the product."

MIKE: "I can take 20% off the price."

RON: "I'm not interested in the product."

Continue until Mike finally gives up.

- Respond to a request in a professional manner. Never
let personalities influence your response or the way
you deliver your response. Respond to the request,
not the person. Also, always respond as firmly,
calmly, and unemotionally as possible. The word
"no" can cause negative feelings. Don't intensify
the situation by using a loud voice or harsh words.

The above guidelines are general rules. The following cases present more specific situations and will equip you with additional techniques for *assertively* saying "no."

DENYING SALARY REQUESTS

Janet accepted a secretary position in a real estate office six months ago. Although the starting pay was lower than she wanted, Barry, her boss, informed her that she would be given a performance review after six months. Barry also indicated that she would be given a five percent increase if her performance was "above standard." Unfortunately, Janet's job performance during the past six months has not been "above standard." In fact, it has been "below standard." First, she has been late to work numerous times. Second, she types extremely fast and makes many typing errors. And, she does not carefully proofread her typing output. Third, she has forgotten to give Barry several important phone messages. Janet recently reminded Barry that she had been on the job six months and asked for a five percent pay raise. Barry promptly scheduled her performance review:

"Janet, I am very pleased with your job performance in several areas. You interface extremely well with our customers. I have received several compliments on your courteous and professional manner. You do an excellent job of answering their questions and following up on open issues. You have also established a good rapport with the agents in our office. You respond to their requests in a timely manner and always go the extra mile in helping them close business. In addition, I am also pleased with the weekly sales meetings. You have done a superb job coordinating the agenda and sales information."

"Janet, although your job performance is excellent in these areas, I am disappointed in several other areas. You have been late to work eight times during the past six months. I understand that unexpected situations can occasionally occur in the morning; however, you only gave me a satisfactory explanation for two of these occurrences. You have also forgotten to give me several important phone messages. Phone messages are extremely important in our business. Unreturned phone calls can result in lost sales. Finally, I am disappointed in the quality of your typing. You need to do a much better job of proofreading your typing before you give it to me. Janet, these are not new issues. I have counseled you on these issues several times during the past six months."

"Janet, considering all of these issues, your present level of performance does not merit a salary increase. Before I consider giving you a raise, I need to see significant improvement in all of these areas. You must be at work on time every morning unless you have a valid excuse. You must carefully record all my phone messages and give them to me in a timely manner. And, you must improve the quality of your typing and proofreading. I know you have a heavy workload, but you must allocate more time to proofreading. It is a high priority. Janet, if you focus on improving these areas, I am confident that you can bring your performance to a level that will merit an increase in pay. You are a valuable member of our team, and we all want to see you succeed."

Barry did an excellent job of *assertively* saying "no" to Janet. This case demonstrates several important techniques.

First, Barry used the *sandwich technique* very effectively. He conveyed positive messages before and after the denial. In the beginning of the performance review he discussed the areas where Janet's performance was excellent. Then, he pointed out the areas where Janet needed to improve. And finally, he closed on a positive note by telling her that he was confident that she could bring her performance to a level that would merit an increase in the future. He also informed her that she was a valuable member of the team.

Second, Barry outlined, very specifically, the areas that Janet needed to improve on. He also explained why these areas were important to him and the company.

Third, Barry did not "surprise" Janet in the meeting with new performance issues. He reminded her that he had counseled her on these issues several times during the past six months. This tendency to "hold back," and then "surprise," is a common characteristic of passive/aggressive managers. They silently document negative behavior during the review period and wait until the actual review to "unload" on the employee.

Fourth, Barry informed Janet in a professional and unemotional manner that her present level of performance did not merit a salary increase. Remember, denying pay increases can cause negative feelings. Always respond as firmly, calmly, and unemotionally as possible.

The above case presents a situation where an employee does not deserve a pay increase. Unfortunately, there are other situations where employees do warrant a pay increase, but their managers are unable to approve the requests. The following cases will equip you with additional techniques to help you handle these challenging situations.

Tim, a computer support technician, accepted a job at a regional bank four months ago. Bob, his supervisor, is extremely happy with his performance. Although Tim has been there only four months, he is trouble-shooting problems that took the other technicians several years to learn. Bob, recognizing Tim's outstanding trouble-shooting ability, has started to assign him some of the most difficult problems. Tim, also recognizing his value, recently asked Bob for a pay increase. This placed Bob in a very difficult position. Although Tim's performance is exceptional, bank policy does not allow salary reviews before one year of employment. Here is Bob's response to Tim's request:

"Tim, I am very pleased with your job performance. In fact, in four short months, you have become one of the best trouble-shooters in the group. Although I would like to give you an increase now, bank policy requires one year of employment before the first salary review. However, since you are such an outstanding employee, I approached my boss and asked for an exception to the policy. She agreed to reduce the one year period to six months. Therefore, I have been authorized to give you a salary review in two months. Assuming that you maintain your excellent performance, I will do everything I can to get you an increase at that time."

The above case demonstrates that salary issues are not always black and white. There is plenty of room for compromise and negotiation in the gray area. Fortunately, Bob is an assertive manager and was not afraid to ask his boss for what he wanted. In addition to adjusting the review period, there are several other alternatives to saying "no" to a salary request. You can compromise and offer a reduced amount. Or, you can offer some other benefit such as stock options or additional paid vacation. These options are often used during tight budgets.

The following case depicts the most difficult salary issue. A deserving employee comes to you requesting a salary increase, but you just don't have the money.

"Eileen, I agree that you deserve a raise. Your job performance is excellent, and you are one of the hardest working employees in the company. Unfortunately, sales are soft this quarter and management has temporarily suspended salary reviews. However, sales opportunities look good next quarter, and I am confident that the company will be back on track soon. I will get back with you in three months and review your request. Please continue your outstanding effort, and help us work through this challenging time. Thank you for all your hard work and dedication."

You have to walk a fine line in this situation. You must be honest about the financial health of the company. However, if you paint too bleak a picture, the employee may look to another company for job security. Try to be realistic, but give the employee hope for the future.

DENYING PROMOTION REQUESTS

Denying a request for a promotion is often more difficult than turning down a request for a raise. Promotion denials often trigger a much stronger emotional response. Employees often perceive this as a dead-end to their career path and begin to question their future with the company. When employees are denied promotions, they usually react in one of three ways.

First, they may turn the rejection inward and blame themselves for not getting the promotion. They beat themselves up and dwell on all the things they should have done better in the past. This self-defeating behavior is frequently accompanied by depression and often leads to further erosion of their self-esteem and self-confidence.

Second, they may turn the rejection outward and blame their boss for the loss of the promotion. "Dave does not understand or appreciate my accomplishments." "I always knew that Dave liked Bill better than me." "This is just another example of Dave's incompetence." Although this "sour grapes" reaction is better than turning the reaction inward, it often negatively impacts the employee's attitude and future job performance.

Third, they may accept the situation for what it is. They congratulate the person being promoted and tell their boss how much they appreciate being considered for the position. In addition, they inform their boss that they are interested in future opportunities and ask what additional training or education will help them advance in their career. Obviously, this is the healthiest reaction.

It's difficult to predict what type of reaction you will get when you inform an employee that he or she did not get the promotion. However, you can minimize adverse reactions if you adhere to the following suggestions:

- Notify the employee as soon as possible.
  Never let an employee find out from someone
  else that he or she did not get the position.

- Deny a promotion request in a professional and unemotional manner. These situations are more emotional than salary requests because of career implications.

- Use the sandwich technique to minimize the employee's disappointment. Use complimentary statements before and after the promotion denial.

- Give the employee a full explanation why
  he or she did not get the promotion.

- Refrain from being apologetic or defensive. You have carefully examined the qualifications of all the candidates and have made the best decision.

- Give the employee hope for the future.
  Suggest ways that the employee can improve
  his or her qualifications for future opportunities
  by additional experience, training, or education.

Susan is a nurse who has worked in a metropolitan hospital for the past five years. She recently applied for a supervisor position in the pediatric section. Cheryl, the hiring manager, interviewed Susan and four other candidates for the position. Unfortunately, Susan did not get the position. Here is Cheryl's response to Susan:

"Susan, you are an excellent candidate for a supervisor position. Your annual performance reviews are outstanding and your people skills are superb. Also, your current supervisor feels that you have all the ingredients to make a successful supervisor. However, I have decided to place Linda in this position because her qualifications are a little stronger than yours. It was a difficult decision because both of you are so exceptional. Susan, you have a bright future at this hospital. To help you advance in your career, I encourage you to enroll in some of the hospital-sponsored management training classes. There are several excellent classes designed for nurses who are considering management responsibility."

The above case demonstrates many of the guidelines for assertively denying promotion requests. The following case adds a new twist—the seniority issue.

Randy is an accounts payable clerk in a manufacturing plant. He has been in this job for six years and is currently looking for a new position with more responsibility. One of Randy's friends in the payroll section recently informed him that the supervisor of that section was going to retire next month. Randy confirmed the retirement and made an appointment with Greg, the accounting manager, to interview for the position. The interview went like this:

"Randy, I really appreciate your interest in the payroll supervisor position. I have reviewed your annual performance reviews and have talked with your current supervisor. Although you are qualified for the position, there are several other applicants, with more seniority, who are also qualified. Company policy is very clear in this situation. When two or more employees with comparable qualifications apply for a position, the decision is guided by seniority status. Considering the seniority policy, it would be inappropriate and unfair to select you over others whose qualifications are comparable to yours. Randy, keep up the excellent work. I am going to personally monitor your career

174

here and promise to bring you along as fast as I can. In addition, I'm going to talk to your current supervisor about increasing the responsibilities in your present job."

In the above case, Greg's hands were tied by company policy. He could not promote Randy to the position. However, he did do a good job of using the sandwich technique to assertively deny the promotion request.

Seniority policies can be extremely frustrating for managers and employees. Subjective interpretation of these policies, as well as faulty assessment of candidate qualifications, often leads to less qualified employees being promoted. Unfortunately, many excellent employees leave companies due to this problem.

DENYING SCHEDULE CHANGES

One of the greatest challenges facing supervisors is scheduling employees, particularly part-time employees. Many companies, especially retail establishments, rely heavily on part-time workers. They save a considerable amount of money not having to pay fringe benefits such as health insurance and retirement. In addition, part-time employees are ideal for covering peak business times. Unfortunately, many part-time employees have other responsibilities that often conflict with work schedules. The following case demonstrates this situation.

Pam is a sophomore in college and has worked part-time at a local department store for the past two years. Helen, her boss, considers her an excellent employee and has given her several pay increases. Pam recently joined the college volleyball team, and the weekly games now conflict with her work schedule. In order to resolve this issue, she approached Helen and requested that her schedule be changed next week. Here is Helen's response to Pam's request:

"Pam, I am delighted that you made the volleyball team. I have always felt that sports are an important part of a balanced life style. Although I've approved your request for a schedule change, I cannot implement it until next month. It would not be fair to the other employees to change the department schedule on such short notice. In the meantime, why don't you work out a time trade with one of your coworkers? I can approve that on short notice. Pam, you are a valued member of this group. I'm confident that we can find a way to resolve this issue. Please keep me updated on the status of the time trade."

Once again, notice how the sandwich technique is used to assertively deny the request. Also, notice how Helen proposes an alternative and makes a sincere effort to work with Pam. Excellent part-time employees, like Pam, often require flexibility on their manager's part to resolve scheduling issues.

DENYING TIME-OFF REQUESTS

Another scheduling issue that supervisors face involves approving, and denying, time-off requests. Although time-off policies vary from company to company, most organizations give their full-time employees a certain number of days off per year. This paid time-off is in addition to paid holidays. Many companies lump vacation time and sick leave into one bucket and call it personal time-off (PTO). For example, an employee may accrue 16 hours of PTO for every 160 hours worked. Employees are responsible for monitoring their PTO balance and should maintain a sufficient balance for emergencies. Although employees are encouraged to take time-off to avoid "burn-out," supervisors may not be in a position to automatically approve every request. Here are some typical situations when the request may be denied:

First, it may be an unreasonable request. If the employee has been taking excessive time-off during the past few months, perhaps it is time for the employee to focus on more important things—like his or her job! Obviously, if the employee has a valid emergency situation, you should give him or her the time-off.

Second, it may be a bad time to approve anyone's time-off. If the business is seasonal, everyone may have to work during peak times. Or, if its flu season, and you are down several employees, you may have to deny time-off requests. In fact, you may have to cancel previously approved time-off.

Third, another employee may have already requested time-off for the same period. If you have already approved a previous request, you may have to deny the current one.

Fourth, if the employee's PTO bank is near empty, you should deny the request unless it is an emergency. Although it's the employee's responsibility to monitor the PTO balance, sometimes supervisor intervention is required to make the employee aware of the situation.

Mary is a dispatcher in a county government 9-1-1 center. She has been on the job six months and has just completed the training program. Her monthly training reviews are outstanding, and she is now certified to operate all radio channels without supervision. Mary plans to get married next month and has requested ten days (80 hours PTO) off. Although she has accumulated 96 hours in her PTO bank, Joan, her supervisor, has several concerns:

"Mary, we are all delighted about your upcoming wedding. We wish you much happiness and success. I've reviewed your request for 80 hours PTO and have several concerns. First, you only have 96 hours in your PTO bank. If I approve 80 hours off, that will leave a balance of only 16 hours. That doesn't leave you much time for possible illnesses or other emergencies. In addition, you have been here only six months. Although your training reviews are outstanding, you need consistent, uninterrupted experience to reinforce your training. A full two week interruption at this time will have a negative impact on your development as a dispatcher. I understand the importance of your PTO request. However, considering these important issues, I can only approve 40 hours at this time. In three months, after you have accumulated more dispatcher experience, and PTO, I would be willing to approve an additional 40 hours off."

"Mary, you have the potential of becoming an excellent dispatcher. You have worked hard during the past six months and have accomplished many goals. I am confident that you will continue to excel and have a very rewarding career."

Joan did an excellent job of assertively denying Mary's request, under very difficult circumstances. It's not easy telling an employee that she can't take two weeks off for her honeymoon. How did Joan accomplish this task? First, she used the sandwich technique very effectively. Second, she explained why she couldn't approve the full 80 hours at this time. Third, she offered a reasonable alternative to the request. And fourth, she responded to the request in a professional and empathetic manner.

DENYING UNREASONABLE PERKS

Steve wants a new computer. Betty wants new office furniture. And Ken wants to attend a conference in Hawaii. Sound familiar? Managers are flooded with requests like these every day. Sometimes they are justifiable. In other cases they are nothing more than unreasonable perks. Shy managers often approve unreasonable perks just to keep their employees happy. They're afraid if they deny these requests their employees won't like them. Although this passive approach may keep everyone happy in the short run, it is a recipe for disaster in the long run. Budgets are not unlimited. Eventually, the well will run dry and the manager won't have the money to fund these insatiable wants. Also, employees may appear to be happy with a boss who can't say "no," but ultimately they will lose respect for the manager and label him or her as a pushover.

Responses to unreasonable perks should not include lengthy excuses, justifications, or rationalizations. After all, the request is unreasonable. However, the response should avoid the appearance of an arbitrary "no." Whenever possible, try to include in your message a short assessment of real need versus cost. Here are some assertive responses to the above requests:

- "Steve, I've reviewed your request for a new computer and have decided not to approve it at this time. Your current computer is only two years old and is still adequate for your job requirements."

- "Betty, I've reviewed your request for new office furniture and have decided not to approve it at this time. Your current furniture is in excellent condition and is still adequate for your job requirements."

- "Ken, I've reviewed your request to attend the conference in Hawaii and have decided not to approve it. Although there are several good topics on the agenda, I feel the excessive cost of this trip outweighs the potential benefits."

DENYING PROPOSALS AND SUGGESTIONS

Encouraging open communication with your subordinates is extremely important. It is the cornerstone of participative management. Denying proposals and suggestions must be handled very carefully. On the one hand, if you constantly approve questionable proposals, the consequences can be devastating to the company and your career. On the other hand, if you constantly reject questionable proposals, you may cut off communication from your staff. Here are some suggestions to help you navigate this minefield:

First, always discuss significant subordinate proposals with your entire staff. You may have an initial negative reaction to a proposal. However, your staff may have a positive reaction. Eventually, they may help you see the benefits and potential of the proposal. Remember, participative management is the key to an effective management process.

Second, discussions concerning proposals should always focus on the proposal, not the person sponsoring it. Keep the discussion focused on the advantages and disadvantages of the proposal. Don't let personalities influence the right decision.

Third, most proposals can often be refined and improved. If the proposal has potential, assign a team to "brainstorm" the idea and refine the proposal.

Fourth, consider the timing of the proposal. Timing is often a factor in accepting, or rejecting, a proposal. Budget constraints, project priorities, reorganization, and other business conditions may affect the timing of a proposal. A good idea may be rejected because now is not the right time to implement it. Don't discard the proposal. Put it on the shelf and bring it back when the time is right.

Although many proposals have some merit, and can be refined to benefit the company, there are some proposals that are just bad ideas. These will be quickly recognized by your staff and politely disposed of. However, you will have to deal with minor suggestions that lack merit. You can address these situations individually and assertively deny these suggestions using the techniques discussed in this chapter.

EXERCISE 9.1

Make a list of the eight guidelines for saying "no" presented at the beginning of this chapter. Place this list in the top middle drawer of your desk. Review this list before you respond to a subordinate request. (This should not be a problem since the first guideline instructs you to give yourself time to evaluate the request.) Keep a logbook on all subordinate requests. Record the request and your response. If you responded with a "no," give yourself a grade on each of the nine guidelines. If you responded with a "yes," when you really wanted to say "no," go back and read this chapter again! When your logbook indicates progress on learning how to say "no," give yourself a reward.

SAYING NO TO YOUR PEERS

Saying "no" to your peers is more difficult than saying "no" to your subordinates. As you learned in the last chapter, your success as a manager depends on your ability to effectively interact with other managers and departments. Many of your tasks and projects require the assistance of these managers. If you alienate them, your project is doomed from the start. These managers are going to assertively ask you for what they want, and they don't want to hear you say "no."

Considering the importance of these peer relationships, how do you assertively deny their requests? In most cases, you can use the same guidelines outlined for subordinates. However, here are several important modifications:

First, try to avoid an absolute denial. Propose an alternative time, schedule, resource, or any other compromise to avoid an absolute denial.

Second, offer a complete explanation for not being able to accommodate the original request, even when you propose an alternative. Most peers will understand that you have limited time and resources and will be receptive to compromise solutions.

Third, unlike subordinate situations, it is appropriate to be apologetic and say, "I'm sorry," when you can't accommodate the original request. This will not be considered a sign of weakness.

Fourth, try to balance your peer denials. Don't accept most of the requests from one peer and constantly reject requests from another. Warning! Don't get in the bad habit of doing favors for certain peers just because they do favors for you. Try to improve the relationships with peers who tend to reject your requests.

Although you should always try to find an alternative solution, there will be times when you have no choice but to deny a peer request. In these cases, be apologetic, use the sandwich technique, and offer a thorough explanation of why you can't accommodate the request. If the peer becomes aggressive and will not take "no" for an answer, you may have to switch to the broken record response.

SAYING NO TO YOUR BOSS

How can you say "no" to your boss? After all, he or she has the authority to terminate you, or discipline you for insubordination. Nevertheless, when you strongly believe that you are right, you have a responsibility to your company, your boss, and yourself, to disagree with your manager. However, anytime you disagree with your boss you are taking a risk. You can minimize this risk if you follow these suggestions:

- Develop a foundation of accountability and trust with your manager before you seek to assert yourself on any issue. The tips for laying this foundation were presented in the last chapter.

- Set your priorities and "pick your battles." Don't disagree with every minor issue. If you do, you'll be looking for a new job soon.

- Schedule your meeting right after a favorable event, when your boss is in a good mood. Timing is everything.

- Look and act assertive. Make direct eye contact, keep your head up, shoulders back, and hands relaxed or gesturing normally. Speak with authority and use clear, resonant tones.

- Do your homework and develope proposals compatible with your manager's communication style. If your boss likes quantitative analysis, present your supporting documentation on charts and graphs.

- Ask for permission to disagree with your manager. For example: "I have some concerns about the production schedule. Can we discuss them?"

- Refrain from using words or phrases like "no," "I can't," or "I disagree." There are many ways you can say "no" without having it sound like "no."

- Disagree with the decision, not your boss. Stress the benefits to the company. Most managers respect someone who is trying to do the right thing for the company.

- Thank your manager at the end of the meeting for the opportunity to express your concerns. If your boss abides by the original decision, even after you have expressed your concerns and offered feasible alternatives, don't beat a dead horse—exit gracefully.

To become an assertive manager, you must learn how to say "no" to your boss. Remember, there are many ways you can say "no" without having it sound like "no." The following cases will demonstrate several of these important techniques.

QUESTIONING UNREALISTIC ASSIGNMENTS

Art supervises maintenance operations for an amusement park in Florida. In addition to major maintenance projects, Art's staff also performs daily preventive maintenance on all the rides. Harry, his manager, has just directed him to refurbish and paint one of the roller coasters. Harry gave Art a deadline of 30 days. After analyzing the scope of work, Art estimates the project will take 60 days. Although Art supervises a group of eight maintenance employees, he is convinced the deadline is unrealistic. He scheduled the following meeting with Harry to express his concerns:

ART: "Harry, I have some concerns about the coaster refurbishment. Can we discuss them?"

HARRY: "Sure, you know I'm always open to constructive feedback."

ART: "After carefully analyzing the scope of work, I believe 30 days is very optimistic. If we push the staff to meet that deadline, I will have to request heavy overtime. In addition, with such a tight schedule, I'm also concerned that quality might be compromised."

HARRY: "Art, you know the importance of minimizing downtime on a major ride. Every day the coaster is down impacts revenue and customer satisfaction."

ART: "I agree that minimizing downtime is an important objective. However, we must also insure that safety is not compromised. Therefore, I have developed two other alternative schedules for your review. The 60 day schedule uses no overtime and no outside contractors. The 45 day schedule uses moderate overtime and an outside contractor for painting."

Harry reviewed the three alternatives and chose the 45-day schedule. Art was successful in gaining approval for his alternative because he assertively questioned Harry's original request. This case reinforces several of the suggestions previously outlined in this section.

First, Art asked for permission to disagree with his manager. He tactfully mentioned that he had some concerns about the project and then asked if he could discuss them.

Second, Art was not confrontational and did not challenge Harry. He didn't use words or phrases like "no," "I can't," or "I disagree."

Third, Art disagreed with the decision, not his boss. He expressed sincere concern for the company by mentioning heavy overtime and possible quality compromises.

Fourth, Art offered Harry feasible alternatives. And, he had the supporting documentation to back up his alternatives.

QUESTIONING INADEQUATE BUDGETS

Robert manages the information technology group in a government agency. Due to increased users and a considerable number of new programming projects, he submitted a 20% increase in his budget request for next year. Unfortunately, management trimmed his request down to a 5% increase. Concerned that he would no longer be able to provide excellent service and support for the agency, he scheduled a meeting with Darlene, his manager. The conversation went like this:

ROBERT: "Darlene, I am very concerned about next year's budget. Can we talk about it?"

DARLENE: "Robert, I know you're disappointed in the latest numbers. I'm not sure I can do anything about it, but we can discuss your concerns."

ROBERT: "If the current numbers hold, it will be very difficult to provide excellent service to all our users next year. The agency has added 60 new users this year and plans to add 80 more next year. In addition, our group has been requested to develop eight new applications next year."

DARLENE: "Robert, I appreciate your concerns, and agree that your group is under a lot of pressure to meet growing demands. I am not the final decision maker on budget issues, but I do have some influence. I will meet with my boss tomorrow and plead your case."

Well, Robert didn't get the full 20% increase that he had originally requested, but he did get 10%. That's better than 5%. Robert improved his budget by fulfilling his responsibility to his company, his boss, and himself. He assertively questioned a management decision that he strongly believed was not the right decision.

QUESTIONING EXCESSIVE TRAVEL

Scott accepted an executive position with a paper company in New York a year ago. During the job interview, he was told the position required 25% travel, since most of the processing plants were in the south. During the first six months, his boss requested him to travel about one week per month. However, during the past six months the travel requests have increased to three weeks per month. This excessive travel is starting to take a toll on his health and his marriage. Seeing no light at the end of the tunnel, Scott decided to question his boss about the excessive travel.

SCOTT: "Alex, I'm concerned about the amount of time I spend traveling. Can we talk about it?"

ALEX: "Well, Scott, when I interviewed you I told you that travel to the plants in the south was an important part of your job."

SCOTT: "Yes, I realize that. But, you indicated that the position required 25% travel. During the past six months you have requested me to travel 75% of the time. Is this a new job requirement, or will the travel decrease back to the 25% level that I experienced during the first six months?"

ALEX: "Scott, I had no idea that you were traveling that much. Thank you for bringing this to my attention. I assure you that the travel requests will be greatly reduced in the future."

As Alex was talking to Scott, his nose grew longer and longer. Of course he knew how much Scott was traveling. He was the one requesting it. However, Alex did keep his promise. For the next three months he reduced Scott's travel to 50%. Although Scott was not happy with the 50% travel, he felt Alex was moving in the right direction. Unfortunately, Alex did an about-face during the fourth month and increased Scott's travel back to 75%. This did not surprise Scott. During his short tenure with the company, he learned that Alex had a reputation for "burning people out." Scott decided that enough was enough. During the next few months he called in sick several times and canceled trips. During these times he interviewed with several companies and eventually found a position that required less travel.

EXERCISE 9.2

Review this section before you schedule a meeting to disagree with your boss. Keep a journal on all of the requests that you decide to question. Record the request and the outcome. What techniques were successful? In what areas do you need to improve? Reward yourself for documented progress in questioning requests that you don't agree with.

CHAPTER HIGHLIGHTS

- Shy managers have a difficult time using the word "no." They allow themselves to be manipulated by guilt, anger, and tears. To become an assertive manager, you must learn how to say "no" to your subordinates, your peers, and your superiors.

- Before you respond to a request, you must give yourself time to carefully study and research all aspects of the request.

- Once you decide to deny a request, you must plan your response. If you hesitate during your response, you will project uncertainty and may open the door for a challenge.

- Always use assertive body language when denying a request. If you say "no" with your words and "maybe" with your body, the person will believe your body and challenge your response.

- If you cannot agree to a request, try to find an alternative. This could be an alternate time for the meeting or an alternate resource for the project.

- If you respond with a "no," and can't offer an alternative, then briefly clarify your reasons. However, do not include lengthy excuses, justifications, or rationalizations.

- Use the broken record response when dealing with very aggressive or manipulative people who "won't take no for an answer." Select a brief statement and calmly repeat it after each request.

- Saying "no" to your peers is more difficult than saying "no" to your subordinates. Your success as a manager depends on your ability to effectively interact with other managers and departments. These managers are going to assertively ask you for what they want, and they don't want to hear you say "no."

- Saying "no" to your boss can be a very risky proposition. After all, he or she has the authority to terminate you or discipline you for insubordination. Nevertheless, when you strongly believe that you are right, you have a responsibility to your company, your boss, and yourself to disagree with your manager.

- When disagreeing with your boss, you must (1) develop a foundation of accountability and trust, (2) set your priorities and "pick your battles," (3) select a time when your boss is in a good mood, (4) look and act assertive, (5) play to your manager's communication style, (6) ask for permission to disagree, (7) never use words or phrases like "no," "I can't," or "I disagree," and (8) disagree with the decision, not your boss.

10

CORRECTING EMPLOYEE BEHAVIOR

When your employees come to work late, do you tend to "look the other way?" When they fail to turn in assignments on time, do you frequently give them "the benefit of the doubt?" And, when they have conflicts and verbally abuse each other, do you often ignore the situation "in hopes it will go away?" If you answered "yes" to any of these questions, you may have a problem correcting employee behavior.

Employees are not perfect. Even experienced workers make mistakes. Managers and supervisors have to deal with a vast array of unwanted behaviors every day. Here are some of the most common:

- Coming to work late

- Leaving work early

- Taking too much time on breaks

- Taking excessive unscheduled leave

- Failing to follow policies and procedures

- Failing to meet goals and objectives

- Making too many mistakes

- Turning in incomplete assignments

- Turning in assignments late

- Being non-responsive to delegated tasks

- Being rude to coworkers

- Being rude to customers

- Undermining supervisor authority

Shy managers have a difficult time correcting these unwanted behaviors. Their need for approval and fear of rejection inhibit them from addressing employee problems. They have a distorted perception that employees don't want corrective feedback. After all, if you correct an employee's behavior, he or she may resent it. And, worst of all, the employee may stop liking you. Ironically, most employees want just the opposite. They want to be informed if their performance is not up to standards. Employees have nothing to gain by performing below standards, unless they want to be fired.

When shy managers become aware of employee problems, they usually react in one of the following ways:

First, they may simply ignore the problem, in hopes that it will go away. They convince themselves that the problem is not serious and will eventually "blow over," if they wait long enough. Unfortunately, many problems do not "blow over." Instead, they "blow up," usually in the manager's face.

Second, they may switch to the aggressive behavior mode if the problem intensifies and the pressure builds up. In this case, shy managers temporarily transform into aggressive managers and harshly criticize the employee's behavior.

Third, they may deny the solvability of the problem. In

some cases, they turn the rationalization outward and feel the employee situation is just too complex to solve. In other cases, they turn the rationalization inward and convince themselves that they don't have the expertise to solve the problem. In either case, the problem goes unresolved, and the situation usually gets worse.

Fourth, they may give feedback, but it is usually vague and imprecise. Instead of addressing the real issues, they sugar-coat the corrective feedback. This gives employees a false picture of their performance and does little to solve the problem.

Shy managers do their employees a disservice by failing to address problems in their work. Most employees want to be notified when their performance is substandard. They want the opportunity to improve.

BENEFITS OF CORRECTIVE FEEDBACK

Assertive managers, on the other hand, recognize that correcting employee behavior benefits employees in several ways.

First, it gives employees a chance to do something about their problems. Most employees don't want to fail. They want to improve and succeed in their jobs.

Second, it helps employees feel more confident and secure in their jobs. Improved job performance leads to increased productivity, job satisfaction, and security.

Third, it provides employees an opportunity to build a trusting relationship with their boss. Corrective feedback should not be viewed as criticism. Instead, it should be viewed as on-going coaching and on-the-job training.

Assertive managers also realize that correcting employee behavior benefits themselves and the company.

First, reducing substandard performance improves productivity, absenteeism, and turnover. It also improves motivation, morale, and teamwork. In short, it makes the manager and his or her department look good.

Second, employees have more respect for managers who deal with problems. Managers who continue to ignore employee problems eventually lose the respect of their people.

Third, correcting employee behavior gives the manager an opportunity to build a trusting relationship with their employees. If more managers viewed this function as on-going coaching and on-the-job training, the inhibition to correct employee behavior would be greatly reduced.

SETTING EXPECTATIONS AND STANDARDS

How can you correct employee behavior if they don't know what's expected of them? It's your responsibility as a manager to set expectations and clearly communicate performance standards. This process should start on the employee's first day at work. The following suggestions are adapted from Loren Belker's book, *The First-Time Manager*:

- Make sure your employees understand company policies and procedures, especially the ones pertaining to your department. In addition, review any other activities that you deem inappropriate.

- Establish performance standards for every job in your department. These standards should be included in every job description.

- Develop performance standards that are realistic and measurable. They are the objective

yardstick used to measure the quantity
and quality of work performed.

- Make sure that you have methods within your department that allow you to constantly monitor employee performance in relationship to the standards. Feedback is critical to this entire process. You must know as soon as possible when employee performance is substandard so that you can immediately correct it.

Performance standards vary from company to company. They may also vary within a company. In some organizations, such as manufacturing, they may be defined as units of output or error rates. In other organizations, like sales, they may be expressed in terms of sales volume, growth rates, or market share. Whatever the case, all employees must know what standards they're expected to comply with. Managers who attempt to correct employee behavior on the basis of nebulous work standards are headed for trouble.

GUIDELINES FOR CORRECTING BEHAVIOR

To become an assertive manager, you must learn how to correct unwanted employee behavior. Whether it's coming to work late, handing in an incomplete report, or failing to achieve a sales goal, you must deal with the problem. The following suggestions will help you assertively correct unwanted employee behavior:

- Choose an appropriate place and time for the
  meeting. Always meet one-on-one in a private setting.
  Also, make sure this is a good time for you and
  the employee. The corrective feedback will be less

effective if either of you are stressed or distracted.

- Plan what you want to say and how you want to communicate it. Document your issues and make thorough notes for the meeting.

- Look and act assertive. Make direct eye contact, keep your head up, shoulders back, and hands relaxed or gesturing normally. Speak with authority, and use clear resonant tones.

- Start the meeting off on a positive note. Give the employee some positive feedback on what you do like about his or her behavior.

- Conduct the meeting with a coaching attitude, and encourage the employee to participate in the conversation. Use open-ended questions to draw the employee out. It's important that the employee be allowed to express his or her viewpoint.

- Direct your comments toward the unwanted behavior, not the person. Never make general statements like, "you're irresponsible," "you're careless," or "you're undependable." The objective of corrective feedback is to change behavior, not personality traits.

- Include a nonjudgmental description of the unwanted behavior and its impact on the company. Always communicate calmly and as unemotional as possible.

The above suggestions are general guidelines. The following cases present specific situations and will provide you with additional techniques for assertively correcting unwanted employee behavior.

CORRECTING PUNCTUALITY PROBLEMS

Ben has been working as a loan processor in a mortgage company a little over six months. During his six month probationary period, he was late to work only once. Ben informed Laura, his manager, that he had a flat tire. However, during the past two weeks, Ben's punctuality has become an issue. He has been late to work four times. Each time, he informed Laura that car problems caused his tardiness. After the fourth incident, Laura asked Ben to come to her office.

LAURA: "Ben, I just want to take a few minutes and congratulate you on successfully completing your probationary period. I would also like to give you some feedback on your job performance. I am very pleased with both the quantity and the quality of the loan applications that you have processed. You interface extremely well with customers and do an excellent job of satisfying their needs. However, I am concerned about your punctuality. During the past two weeks you've been late to work four times. What are you doing to correct this problem?"

BEN: "Laura, I've had a rash of car problems. My car is four years old and has 60,000 miles on it. Every time I turn around it seems like something else breaks and has to be replaced. I'm seriously thinking about trading it in for a newer model."

LAURA: "Well, I can't tell you what to do about your car, but I will tell you that getting to work on time is an important requirement of your job. Your customers expect you to be at your desk

197

at eight o'clock every morning. In addition, it's not fair to your coworkers to allow you to come in at a later time. They are all required to be here by eight. Ben, you must find reliable transportation to work."

BEN: "I fully understand your concerns, and I assure you that the problem will be resolved immediately."

Well, Ben didn't get a new car, but he did resolve the problem. Sometimes employees will test your limits, especially after their probationary period is over. However, Laura assertively answered the challenge and did an excellent job of following the guidelines for correcting unwanted employee behavior.

First, Laura started the meeting off on a positive note by congratulating Ben on the successful completion of his probationary period. She also gave him positive feedback on his loan processing accomplishments and his customer service skills.

Second, Laura used an open-ended question to encourage Ben to participate in the discussion. She specifically asked him what he was going to do to correct the problem.

Third, Laura directed her comments toward the unwanted behavior, not the person. Her objective was to change Ben's behavior, not his personality traits.

Fourth, Laura's feedback included a nonjudgmental description of the unwanted behavior and its impact on the company. She pointed out that Ben's customers expect him to be at work on time. In addition, she also reminded him that it was not equitable for him to be late, while his coworkers had to be on time.

The above case demonstrates one type of punctuality problem. Although coming to work late is a serious problem, there are many other punctuality problems that can't be ignored. They include:

- Coming back late from lunch
- Taking excessive breaks
- Leaving work early
- Turning in assignments late
- Coming to meetings late

Assertive managers address these punctuality problems. They follow the previously discussed guidelines and assertively correct these unwanted behaviors.

CORRECTING PRODUCTIVITY PROBLEMS

Eric has been a sales representative for a document imaging company for three and a half years. During the first three years, he met or exceeded his sales goals every quarter. However, during the past two quarters he has struggled and has failed to meet his numbers. George, his manager, believes that Eric has become too comfortable with his current accounts and needs to develop additional accounts. In hopes of turning this situation around, George asked Eric to meet with him in his office.

GEORGE: "Eric, you have been one of our leading sales representatives for the past three years. You have excellent account control and do an outstanding job of consultative selling. However, during the past two quarters you have not achieved your sales objectives. What do you think the problem is?"

ERIC: "Well, most of my customers are complaining about soft sales and reduced budgets."

GEORGE: "Why do you suppose they are experiencing soft sales? Have you been able to identify a common denominator?"

ERIC: "Most of my accounts are banks, mortgage companies, stock brokers, and other financial institutions. As you know, I've accumulated several years of valuable experience configuring custom document imaging systems for the financial community. I understand their operations and have learned how to talk their language. In fact, most of my new business comes from account references within the financial services sector."

GEORGE: "Eric, it looks like your account portfolio is heavily weighted toward companies associated with financial services. That's good as long as the financial sector is performing well. Apparently, that is no longer the case. What other sectors have you thought about prospecting?"

ERIC: "I've been thinking about the local government sector. Although these organizations appear to be less progressive in document imaging, their budgets are more stable and are affected less by economic fluctuations."

GEORGE: "Eric, I think you're on the right track. The local government sector is more stable. It also has excellent market potential. Although this sector may be less progressive, I believe there is an excellent opportunity for consultative selling. Why don't you start making some cold calls, and we'll review your progress in a few weeks."

Although this case demonstrates many of the guidelines for correcting employee behavior, it highlights the coaching technique. Notice how George used open-ended questions to encourage Eric to bring out the problem himself. Then, once the problem was out on the table, George coached Eric toward a possible solution.

CORRECTING QUALITY PROBLEMS

Ann recently accepted a position as an assembly technician with an electronics manufacturing company. Her first week was spent in a classroom where she learned company policy and procedures. She also received basic training in assembly techniques and procedures. Ann's second week was spent on one of the assembly lines where she received supervised, on-the-job training. During the last two weeks, Ann has been assembling units without direct supervision. Although the quantity of her output is above standards, the quality is below standards. Many of her units are rejected during final testing and inspection and have to be reworked. Fran, Ann's manager, is becoming concerned about Ann's progress. She scheduled the following meeting with Ann in her office:

FRAN: "Ann, now that you have been with us for a month, I'd like to take a few minutes and see how you're doing. How do you feel about your progress?"

ANN: "Well, I feel very comfortable in the job. I had a good trainer."

FRAN: "Do you believe that you're now meeting the standards that we have established for this job?"

ANN: "Yes, I feel I'm doing a good job. In fact, my numbers exceed standards."

FRAN: "How about quality?"

ANN: "I have a few rejects. But, isn't that normal for new hires?"

FRAN: "Ann, that's an interesting observation that you've made about the quality of your work. Yes, it is normal for new hires to have rejects, but your reject rate is four times higher than the standard. At this point, your reject rate should be much lower. Although it's important to meet or exceed quantity standards, you must also meet quality standards. What are you going to do about this problem?"

ANN: "Well, I guess I need to slow down a bit and focus on quality."

This case, like the previous one, demonstrates the importance of using open-ended questions to correct employee behavior. Notice how Fran used a series of open-ended questions to bring out the problem. And, observe how Fran placed the final responsibility for solving the problem squarely on Ann's shoulders: "What are you going to do about this problem?"

CORRECTING NEGATIVE BEHAVIOR

In addition to punctuality, productivity, and quality problems, there are many other unwanted employee behaviors that managers must deal with. Some employees are rude to coworkers and customers. Others are non-responsive to delegated assignments. They have to be asked several times before they perform a task. And, some employees are just plain trouble-makers and like to stir the pot. They gossip about other employees, start unfounded rumors, and constantly complain about everything.

Correcting negative behavior is a challenge for most managers because it often involves dealing with an employee's personality. Warning! Don't fall into the trap of trying to change a personality trait. You can't change a "bad attitude." However, you can try to change a specific behavior associated with the bad attitude. The following case will demonstrate this point.

Tom manages an information technology group. Cindy, one of the programmers, approached Tom and informed him that Max was slandering Don. Max allegedly told her that Don was "incompetent and way over his head" and "should be removed from his position." She also informed Tom that Paul, another programmer in the group, overheard the conversation.

Shortly after Cindy left his office, Tom asked Paul to stop by. He asked Paul if he had recently overheard a conversation between Cindy and Max. Without prompting him, Paul confirmed Max's conversation with Cindy, almost to the word.

After Tom made notes from the meetings with Cindy and Paul, he informed his boss of the situation. He then asked Max to come to his office.

TOM: "Max, one of your coworkers has come to me with an allegation about your behavior."

MAX:	"I bet it's Cindy. She just can't mind her own business."
TOM:	"Max, maintaining a harmonious work environment is everyone's business. Now, I understand that you recently made some comments to Cindy about Don. What exactly did you tell Cindy?"
MAX:	"Well, it was no big deal. I only told her that Don wasn't doing his job. Our network reliability sucks."
TOM:	"Max, that's an interesting statement you've made about the conversation, but two of your coworkers have told me something different. Why do you suppose your information is different from mine?"
MAX:	"Well, I can't remember the details. I was too pissed-off."
TOM:	"Max, is it possible that you told Cindy that Don was incompetent and way over his head and should be removed from his position?"
MAX:	"I can't remember. But, I guess it's possible."
TOM:	"Max, slandering a coworker and creating a hostile work environment is a very serious offense. I would like you to apologize to Don, in front of Cindy and Paul, as soon as possible. Do you have a problem with that?"
MAX:	"No."
TOM:	"Also, I will be writing you up for creating a hostile work environment. This formal repri-

mand will be placed in your permanent personnel file. Do you understand?"

MAX: "Yes."

TOM: "Max, this type of behavior will not be tolerated in this organization. Further behavior of this type will result in more serious discipline, up to, and including, termination. Do you understand?"

MAX: "Yes."

Slandering coworkers and creating a hostile work environment is a very serious matter. Although this slander took place behind the employee's back, everyone in the group knew about it within minutes. Fortunately, Tom addressed the issue swiftly and assertively.

First, Tom immediately realized the seriousness of the allegation and wasted no time starting a supervisory inquiry. Events like this can get out of control very fast in a small work group, and serious personnel conflicts can develop rapidly.

Second, Tom talked to Paul to corroborate Cindy's story. Whenever you confront an employee with an allegation, always attempt to corroborate the allegation with two or more witnesses.

Third, Tom immediately informed his boss about the event. Never let your boss hear about a serious personnel issue from someone else.

Fourth, Tom felt no need to use the sandwich technique or give Max positive feedback in the beginning of the conversation. These techniques are not appropriate in situations involving serious employee misconduct.

Fifth, Tom used a series of open-ended questions in an attempt to encourage Max to be responsible and accountable for his behavior. Although Max initially danced around the questions, he eventually acknowledged his negative behavior and the consequences.

Sixth, due to the seriousness of the incident, Tom ended the conversation with a "zero tolerance" message and set the stage for *progressive discipline.* (Note: Max was involved in a similar incident six months later and was terminated.)

PROGRESSIVE DISCIPLINE

Correcting employee behavior can turn into progressive discipline when the unwanted behavior continues. Most companies have a progressive discipline policy to ensure that all employees receive equitable treatment. The consequences for unwanted behavior are outlined in a progressive schedule of disciplinary actions. A typical progressive discipline schedule is presented below:

Occurrence	Disciplinary Action
First	Verbal counseling
Second	Written reprimand
Third	Suspension without pay
Fourth	Demotion
Fifth	Termination

The above schedule is a general guideline for most minor problems. In some cases, the disciplinary action can be more severe than verbal counseling for the first occurrence. For example, an employee may be given a written reprimand, or several days off without pay, for the first occurrence of creating a hostile work environment. Or, an employee may be demoted, or even terminated, for the first occurrence of insubordination.

Correcting employee behavior should be approached with a coaching attitude. However, when the unwanted behavior occurs again and again, the coaching attitude frequently turns to "CYA." In this age of "employee rights" legislation, and "wrongful termination" lawsuits, coaching often takes a back seat to creating a water tight "paper trail." When management discovers that an employee "is not working out," the progressive discipline policy often provides the vehicle for effective termination.

CORRECTING MANAGER BEHAVIOR

So far, this chapter has focused on correcting *employee* behavior. However, managers are also employees and are not immune from making mistakes. All of the unwanted employee behaviors listed in the beginning of this chapter also apply to supervisors and managers. For example, some managers may fail to follow a policy or procedure. Others may not meet their goals or objectives. And, some may be rude and condescending to their peers and employees. Although these individuals are managers, their superiors can't ignore these unwanted behaviors. It is their responsibility to effectively monitor and correct inappropriate manager behavior.

All of the guidelines outlined in the beginning of this chapter also apply to correcting manager behavior. The following case will demonstrate this point.

Alice was recently promoted to supervise the cosmetics department in a department store. She was promoted from sales associate to supervisor in the same department. Shortly after announcing her promotion, Martin, her manager, sent her to a three day training class for new supervisors. Although the feedback from her training instructor was excellent, Martin is concerned about Alice's transition from worker to supervisor. He has frequently observed her taking breaks and going out to lunch with her employees. He has also noticed that Alice tends to ignore inappropriate employee behavior on the sales floor. On several occasions, he has observed sales associates in her department joking and kidding around while frustrated customers were waiting for assistance. In addition, he has discovered unattended cosmetic counters several times during lunch and dinner periods. He suspects that Alice is either scheduling too many employees during the same period or not enforcing time limits. These, as well as other "red flags," have prompted Martin to meet with Alice.

MARTIN: "Alice, now that you've had a few weeks to get your feet wet, how do you feel in your new role?"

ALICE: "Well, I guess I'm kind of overwhelmed with all the new responsibilities. I enjoy making the merchandising decisions but feel awkward when I have to ask someone to do something."

MARTIN: "What did your training instructor say about the transition from worker to supervisor? Did she offer any suggestions or tips?"

ALICE: "Yes, she said it was very important for me to hold a meeting with my group as soon as possible and talk about my new role as supervisor. She also said I should discuss, very specifically, what management expects of me and what I expect from the group."

MARTIN: "Have you had this discussion with your group?"

ALICE: "No, not yet. I didn't want to come on too strong in the beginning and have the group think that this promotion has gone to my head."

MARTIN: "Alice, do you think the group perceives you more as a coworker than a supervisor?"

ALICE: "They all know that I'm the new supervisor. I schedule their hours and sign their time sheets. We all work well together."

MARTIN: "It's important that you all work well together. But, on several occasions I have observed sales associates in your department joking and kidding around while frustrated customers were waiting for service. I have also observed unattended cosmetic counters during lunch and dinner periods. What are you going to do about these problems?"

ALICE: "Well, I guess things have been a little relaxed since I became supervisor. I will hold a group meeting tomorrow and discuss my new role as supervisor."

Notice how Martin used the coaching technique to bring out the problem. Instead of immediately confronting Alice with the inappropriate sales associate behavior, and the unattended cosmetic counters, he asked her a series of open-ended questions to encourage her to discover the problem for herself.

Being promoted from worker to supervisor in the same department can be a stressful challenge. Although Alice has been placed in this difficult situation, she must quickly embrace her new responsibilities if she is to be successful. When talking to the group, she should first focus on the advantages of her being promoted, compared to someone from outside the department. She already knows the cosmetics retail business and the people in the group. In addition, she understands company policies and procedures as well as the company culture. Alice should also remind the group how well they have all worked together in the past.

Alice must then turn the discussion toward her new role as supervisor. She must be honest and tell them that she is going to have to make decisions that some of them won't like. In her new role, there will be times when she will have to deny vacation requests, correct employee behavior, and implement new policies that may not be popular. Also, she will have to support upper-management decisions, even when she doesn't agree with them, because she is now part of management.

In closing the meeting, Alice should thank the group for the excellent working relationship that they all shared in the past. And, she should ask them for their support in her new role so the group may continue to be successful in the future.

EXERCISE 10.1

Make a list of the seven guidelines for correcting employee behavior. Place this list in the top middle drawer of your desk. Review this list before you schedule a corrective meeting. Keep a logbook on all meetings. After each meeting is over, give yourself a grade on each of the seven guidelines. Reward yourself for documented progress in correcting employee behavior.

CHAPTER HIGHLIGHTS

- Shy managers have a difficult time correcting unwanted employee behavior. Their need for approval and fear of rejection inhibit them from addressing employee problems.

- Shy managers have a distorted perception that employees don't want corrective feedback. Ironically, most employees want just the opposite. They want to be informed if their performance is not up to standards.

- When shy managers become aware of employee problems they often (1) ignore the problem in hopes that it will go away, (2) switch to the aggressive behavior mode if the problem intensifies, (3) deny the solvability of the problem, or (4) give vague and imprecise feedback.

- Assertive managers recognize that correcting employee behavior benefits employees because it (1) gives them a chance to do something about their problems, (2) helps them feel more confident and secure in their jobs, and (3) provides them with an opportunity to build a trusting relationship with their boss.

- Assertive managers also realize that correcting employee behavior benefits them and the company because it (1) reduces substandard performance and improves productivity, absenteeism, and turnover, (2) increases employee respect for them because they deal with problems, and (3) gives them an opportunity to build trusting relationships with their employees.

- Managers can't correct employee behavior if the employees don't know what's expected of them. Managers must set expectations and clearly communicate performance standards.

- When correcting employee behavior, assertive managers (1) choose an appropriate place and time for the meeting, (2) plan what they want to say and how they want to say it, (3) look and act assertive, (4) start the meeting off on a positive note, (5) use coaching techniques and open-ended questions, (6) direct their comments toward the unwanted behavior, not the person, and (7) include a nonjudgmental description of the unwanted behavior and its impact on the company.

- Correcting employee behavior can turn into progressive discipline when the unwanted behavior continues. The consequences for unwanted behavior are outlined in a progressive schedule of disciplinary actions.

- When management discovers that an employee "is not working out," the progressive discipline policy often provides the vehicle for effective termination.

- Managers are also employees and are not immune from making mistakes. Some managers may fail to follow a policy or procedure. Others may not meet their goals or objectives. And, some may be rude and condescending to their peers and employees.

- Superiors can't ignore unwanted manager behavior. It is their responsibility to effectively monitor and correct inappropriate manager behavior.

11

THE ASSERTIVE MANAGER

When you walk into a room full of managers you'll have no trouble identifying assertive ones. They will walk up to you, look you directly in the eyes, introduce themselves, and greet you with a firm handshake. They will talk to you with a level, well-modulated voice and attempt to find topics of shared interest. And, they will listen actively and effectively when you speak. You will be drawn to their open and honest approach and anxious to exchange ideas with them. What makes these managers so charismatic? And, why are they so unique?

Assertive managers have learned how to control their thoughts and feelings. They choose to have positive thoughts and feel secure and confident. They accept full responsibility for their feelings and do not blame others for how they feel. In addition, they don't procrastinate or rationalize when faced with situations that are unpleasant or difficult. Instead, they are action-oriented and confront problems at the time they happen.

Assertive managers have high self-esteem. They don't engage in self-denunciation. You won't hear them complaining about themselves, constantly rejecting compliments, or giving credit to others when it really belongs to them. And, you won't see them seeking approval. They have learned that *wanting* approval is healthy, but *needing* approval is self-defeating. In short, assertive managers *like* who they are. They like their physical appearance. They like their intelligence. And, they like their personalities.

Assertive managers have self-confidence. They have learned how to take risks and develop self-confidence in both their personal lives and their professional lives. Both involve setting realistic goals and then breaking them down into manageable tasks. Assertive managers confront and solve problems instead of worrying about them. They minimize their risk of failure in making decisions by thoroughly documenting, researching, and analyzing the problem. In addition, they practice participative management to refine alternative solutions and assure the best possible decision.

Assertive managers have excellent social skills. They have learned how to make small talk, participate in meetings, and make effective presentations. They have mastered the art of small talk and use it effectively to establish new business relationships. They participate in meetings and proactively promote their plans and suggestions. In addition, they are not afraid to speak up in meetings and ask colleagues to clarify their ideas. Assertive managers also make effective presentations. The presentations are well planned and delivered with confidence.

Assertive managers have learned how to ask for what they want. They ask specifically for *what* they want, *when* they want it, and *why* they want it. They are not afraid to assign unpleasant tasks and never let an employee delegate back to them. Assertive managers also ask their peers and their superiors for what they want. They realize that their success as a manager depends on their ability to obtain the necessary support and resources from their peers and their superiors.

Assertive managers have learned how to say "no." They don't allow themselves to be manipulated by guilt, anger, or tears. They are not afraid to deny unwarranted salary requests, untimely schedule changes, or unreasonable perks. Depending on the person and the situation, they use a variety of effective formats for denying requests. Assertive managers have also learned how to *tactfully* disagree with their peers and their superiors. They first ask for permission to disagree and then present several attractive alternatives.

Assertive managers have learned how to correct employee behavior. They don't ignore employee problems, in hopes they will go away. Nor, do they give vague and imprecise feedback and sugar-coat the corrective action. Instead, they use an array of assertive techniques to correct employee behavior. They direct their comments toward the unwanted behavior, not the person. They include a nonjudgmental description of the unwanted behavior and its impact on the company. And, they use coaching techniques and open-ended questions to draw the employee out. All of these assertive techniques facilitate employee participation and accountability.

You have taken a big step toward becoming an assertive manager. You have read this book and successfully completed all of the exercises. However, your journey is not over. Reducing your shyness and increasing your assertiveness is a lifelong project. You must periodically take the Managerial Shyness Survey and monitor your progress. If you find yourself slipping back into your old self-defeating habits, you must reread the appropriate chapter(s) in this book and practice the exercises. Good luck, take care, and keep in touch.

Best regards,
Ron Johnson
www.ronaldjohnson.org

SELECTED REFERENCES

Albright, Mary and Carr, Clay. *101 Biggest Mistakes Managers Make.* Paramus, New Jersey: Prentice Hall, 1997.

Antony, Martin. *10 Simple Solutions to Shyness.* Oakland, California: New Harbinger Publications, 2004.

Axelrod, Alan and Holtje, Jim. *201 Ways to Say No Gracefully and Effectively.* New York: McGraw-Hill, 1997.

Belker, Loren. *The First-Time Manager.* New York: American Management Association, 1993.

Berent, Jonathan. *Beyond Shyness: How to Conquer Social Anxieties.* New York: Fireside, 1994.

Blair, Gerard. "Presentation Skills for Emergent Managers." *IEEE Engineering Management Journal,* December, 1991.

Bower, Sharon and Bower, Gordon. *Asserting Yourself: A Practical Guide for Positive Change.* Reading, Massachusetts: Addison Wesley, 1991.

Braiker, Harriet. *The Disease to Please: Curing the People-Pleasing Syndrome.* New York: McGraw-Hill, 2001.

Branden, Nathaniel. *The Six Pillars of Self-Esteem.* New York: Bantam Books, 1994.

Burley-Allen, Madelyn. *Managing Assertively: How to Improve Your People Skills.* New York: John Wiley & Sons, 1995.

Carducci, Bernardo. *Shyness: A Bold New Approach.* New York: HarperCollins, 1999.

Covey, Stephen. *Seven Habits of Highly Effective People.* New York: Simon & Schuster, 1989.

Davies, Philippa. *Personal Power: How to Become More Assertive and Successful at Work.* London, England: Piatkus Books, 1996.

Drury, Susanne. *Assertive Supervision: Building Involved Teamwork.* Ottawa, Canada: Research Press, 1984.

Dyer, Wayne. *Your Erroneous Zones.* New York: Funk & Wagnalls, 1977.

Enelow, Wendy. "Interview Essentials." *MSN Careers*, July 18, 2003.

Fleming, James. *Become Assertive.* Runcorn, England: David Grant Publishing, 2001.

Leavitt, Harold and Bahrami, Homa. *Managerial Psychology.* Chicago, Illinois: The University of Chicago Press, 1988.

Marshall, Susan. *How to Grow a Backbone: 10 Strategies for Gaining Power and Influence at Work.* Chicago, Illinois: Contemporary Books, 2000.

Martin, Carole. "Ten Interviewing Rules." *MSN Careers*, July 18, 2003.

McKay, Matthew and Fanning, Patrick. *Self-Esteem.* Oakland, California: New Harbinger Publications, 1987.

Nance-Nash, Sheryl. "Asking for a Raise." *Money.net*, January 26, 2001.

Palladino, Connie. *Developing Self-Esteem.* Los Altos, California: Crisp Publications, 1989.

Paterson, Randy. *The Assertiveness Workbook.* Oakland, California: New Harbinger Publications, 2000.

Sahadi, Jeanne. "How to Ask for More Money." *CNN Money*, November 7, 2003.

Schneier, Franklin. *The Hidden Face of Shyness: Understanding & Overcoming Social Anxiety.* New York: Avon Books, 1996.

Smith, Manuel. *When I Say No, I Feel Guilty, Volume II, for Managers and Executives.* Los Angeles, California: A Train Press, 2000.

Stein, Murray and Walker, John. *Triumph Over Shyness: Conquering Shyness and Social Anxiety.* New York: McGraw-Hill, 2003.

Taetzsch, Lyn. *Taking Charge on the Job: Techniques for Assertive Man-*

agement. New York: Executive Enterprises, 1978.

Traub, Gary. "Shyness and Academic Performance." *Psychological Reports* 52, no. 3 (1983).

Zimbardo, Phillip. *Shyness: What It Is, What to Do About It.* Reading, Massachusetts: Addison-Wesley, 1977.

Zucker, Elaina. *The Assertive Manager.* New York: Amacom Books, 1989.

INDEX